BBC

Bitesize

Bitesize

AQA GCSE (9-1)
ENGLISH LANGUAGE

REVISION GUIDE

Series Consultant:
Harry Smith

Author:
Julie Hughes

Contents

How to use this book iii
Your English Language GCSE iv
Paper 1, Question 1 v
Paper 1, Question 2 vi
Paper 1, Question 3 vii
Paper 1, Question 4 viii
Paper 1, Question 5 ix
Paper 2, Question 1 x
Paper 2, Question 2 xi
Paper 2, Question 3 xii
Paper 2, Question 4 xiii
Paper 2, Question 5 xiv

Analysing fiction
Types of fiction text 1
Explicit information 2
Exam skills: Paper 1, Question 1 3
Critical analysis 4
Word classes 5
Words and phrases 6
Inference 7
Connotations 8
Figurative language 9
Sentence forms 10
Reading the question 11
Annotating the text 12
Using evidence 13
Structuring an answer 14
Exam skills: Paper 1, Question 2 15
Structure 16
Openings and endings 17
Sequencing 18
Paragraphs and sentences 19
Narrative perspective 20
Exam skills: Paper 1, Question 3 21
Evaluation 22
Making a judgement 23
Narrative voice 24
Setting 25
Atmosphere 26
Character 27
Exam skills: Paper 1, Question 4 28

Analysing non-fiction
Types of non-fiction text 29
Interpreting unfamiliar vocabulary 30
Skimming and scanning 31
Exam skills: Paper 2, Question 1 32
Synthesising two texts 33
Structuring a synthesis answer 34

Exam skills: Paper 2, Question 2 35
Analysing language 36
Rhetorical devices 37
Tone, style and register 38
Exam skills: Paper 2, Question 3 39
Comparing non-fiction texts 40
Viewpoints 41
Fact, opinion and expert evidence 42
Comparing language 43
Comparing structure 44
Planning a comparative answer 45
Exam skills: Paper 2, Question 4 46

Writing fiction
Audience, purpose and form 47
Vocabulary for effect 48
Figurative language for effect 49
Using sentences for effect 50
Paragraphing 51
Creative openings 52
Creative endings 53
Implying meaning 54
Gathering descriptive ideas 55
Structuring descriptive writing 56
Gathering narrative ideas 57
Structuring narrative writing 58
Exam skills: Narrative writing 59
Exam skills: Descriptive writing 60

Writing non-fiction
Audience, form and purpose 61
Writing for an audience 62
Introductions 63
Conclusions 64
Directing the reader 65
Influencing the reader 66
Rhetorical techniques 67
Using tone, style and register 68
Articles 69
Letters 70
Speeches 71
Essays 72
Leaflets 73
Gathering non-fiction ideas 74
Structuring non-fiction 75
Exam skills: Paper 2, Question 5 76

Writing skills
Beginning a sentence 77
Ending a sentence 78
Commas, semi-colons & colons 79
Other punctuation 80
Parentheses 81
Homophones 82
Common spelling errors 83
Spelling strategies 84
Common grammatical errors 85
Proofreading 86

Spoken Language
Choosing a topic 87
Planning your presentation 88
Delivering your presentation 89
Exam skills: Spoken Language 90

Sources
Source A 91
Source B 92
Source C 93
Source D 94
Source E 95
Source F 96
Source G 97
Source H 98
Source I 99
Source J 100
Source K 101
Source L 102
Source M 103

Answers 104

> ☑ Tick off each topic as you go.

How to use this book

Use the features in this book to focus your revision, track your progress through the topics and practise your exam skills.

Features to help you revise

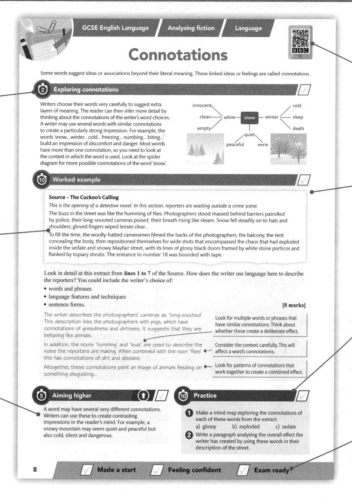

Each bite-sized chunk has a **timer** to indicate how long it will take. Use them to plan your revision sessions.

Reading sources are shown on the page. There are also longer reading sources on pages 91–103 at the back of the book.

Aim higher with special features designed to help you extend your skills and access the top grades.

Scan the **QR codes** to visit the BBC Bitesize website. It will link straight through to more revision resources on that subject.

Worked examples demonstrate how to approach exam-style questions.

Challenge yourself with **practice** at the end of each page and check your answers at the back of the book.

Tick boxes allow you to track the sections you've revised. Revisit each page to embed your knowledge.

Exam focus features

The *About your exam* section at the start of the book gives you all the key information about your exams, as well as showing you how to identify the different questions.

Throughout the topic pages you will also find green *Exam skills* pages. These work through an extended exam-style question and provide further opportunities to practise your skills.

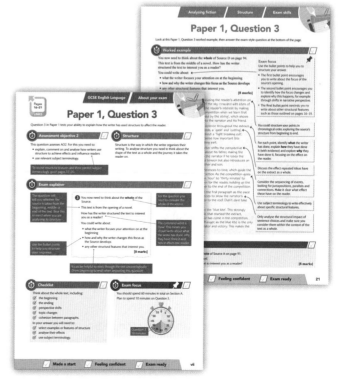

ActiveBook and app

This Revision Guide comes with a **free online edition**. Follow the instructions from inside the front cover to access your ActiveBook.

You can also download the **free BBC Bitesize app** to access revision flash cards and quizzes.

If you do not have a QR code scanner, you can access all the links in this book from your ActiveBook or visit **www.pearsonschools.co.uk/BBCBitesizeLinks**.

Your English Language GCSE

Your GCSE English Language qualification consists of two exam papers, each worth 50% of your GCSE. Each paper tests both reading and writing skills. Speaking and listening skills are also assessed but do not contribute to your overall grade.

⑩ About the exam papers

Each paper is split into two sections, Section A: Reading, and Section B: Writing.

Paper 1:
Explorations in creative reading and writing
1 hour 45 minutes
80 marks

Paper 2:
Writers' viewpoints and perspectives
1 hour 45 minutes
80 marks

In Paper 1, Section A, you will read one **fiction** text from the 20th or 21st century. Spend about 15 minutes reading the text before starting your answers.

In Paper 2, Section A, you will read two **non-fiction** texts. One will be from the 19th century, and one will be from the 20th or 21st century.

In Paper 1, Section B, you will choose between two writing tasks, one of which will be based on a visual stimulus, such as a photo. You could be asked to write either a narrative piece or a description. You must only answer one of these tasks.

In Section B for both papers, you can achieve 24 marks for the content of your answer and 16 marks for the technical accuracy of your spelling, punctuation and grammar.

In Paper 2, Section B, you will be asked to write a non-fiction piece for a specific audience and purpose.

⑤ Exam focus

Practise your reading skills regularly. Try to read something different each day, such as:

- broadsheet and tabloid newspaper articles
- autobiographies, biographies and memoirs
- travel writing
- reviews
- novels and short stories from the 20th and 21st centuries, covering a wide range of genres.

You should focus on:

- identifying the writer's point of view, main ideas and themes
- how the writer uses language to have an effect on the reader. Expand your vocabulary by looking up unfamiliar words and phrases.

Practise your writing skills by using your reading as a stimulus. You could:

- write a letter or article in response to a non-fiction text
- write a short story inspired by the characters or setting of a novel.

② Sections

Sections A and B in both papers are equally weighted and each section carries 40 marks.

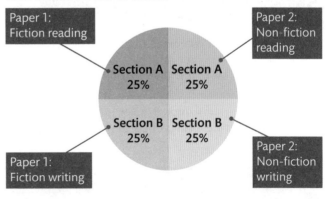

Paper 1:
Fiction reading

Paper 2:
Non-fiction reading

Section A 25%
Section A 25%
Section B 25%
Section B 25%

Paper 1:
Fiction writing

Paper 2:
Non-fiction writing

② My exam dates

Find out the date and time of each of your GCSE English Language exams and write them in this table.

	Date	AM or PM?
Paper 1		
Paper 2		

Paper 1, Question 1

The first question in Paper 1 requires you to retrieve explicit information. This means that you will need to find and quote or paraphrase relevant parts of the text.

2 Reading time

You should start Paper 1 by spending 15 minutes reading the text and questions. You should:

1 read the questions and underline the key words to find out what you need to look for in the source

2 skim read the source to find the main ideas and themes

3 read the source again in more detail, annotating any features that will help you with your answers.

> Go to page 31 to revise skimming.

2 Assessment objective 1

This question assesses the first part of AO1. For this you need to:

- identify explicit information and ideas.

Explicit information is clearly stated and requires no interpretation.

> Go to page 2 to revise explicit information.

2 Command words

Command words are the words used in the exam questions to tell you how you should answer them.

The English Language exam will use the same command words each year, so you should familiarise yourself with them.

2 Exam focus

You should spend 60 minutes in total on Section A. Plan to spend 5 minutes on Question 1.

Reading and planning: 15 minutes

Question 1: 5 minutes

5 Exam explainer

The command word is 'list'. This means you should quote or paraphrase pieces of information from the source. You do not need to write in full sentences or explain your answers.

You will be given a specific topic to focus on.

1 Read again the first part of the Source from **lines 1 to 7**.

List **four** things you learn from this part of the text about the street.

[4 marks]

1 _____

2 _____

3 _____

4 _____

Only give information from the section of the source identified in the question.

There are four marks available. That's one for each correct answer.

Your answers should be concise and clear.

Pages
4–15
LINKS

Paper 1, Question 2

Question 2 in Paper 1 tests your ability to explain how the writer has used language to affect the reader.

 ## Assessment objective 2

This question assesses AO2. For this you need to:

- explain, comment on and analyse how writers use language to achieve effects and influence readers
- use relevant subject terminology.

> To revise language features and their correct subject terminology, go to pages 4–10.

 ## Language

You will be provided with a short extract from the source to analyse. You will need to think about:

- vocabulary choices
- word classes
- connotations
- figurative language
- sentence forms.

 ## Exam focus

You should spend 60 minutes in total on Section A.

Plan to spend 10 minutes on Question 2.

Question 2:
10 minutes

 ## Exam explainer

2 Look in detail at this extract from **lines 1 to 6** of the Source:

> **Source 1 – Even the Dogs**
>
> They break down the door at the end of December and carry the body away.
>
> The air is cold and vice-like, the sky a scouring steel-eyed blue, the trees bleached bone-white in the frosted light of the sun. We stand in a huddle by the bolted door.
>
> The street looks quiet, from here. Steam billows and sighs from a central-heating flue. A television flickers in a room next door. Someone hammers at a fencing post on the far side of the playing fields behind the flats.

How does the writer use language here to describe the street?

You could include the writer's choice of:

- words and phrases
- language features and techniques
- sentence forms. **[8 marks]**

> Only analyse the extract provided.

> The command word is 'how'. This means you should write about what the writer has done, why they have done it and how it affects the reader.

> Use the bullet points to remind yourself of what to look for.

> The focus of the question will change in every paper. Make sure your answer sticks to it.

> Use subject terminology when you identify a feature and provide evidence to support your ideas.

   Made a start   **Feeling confident**   **Exam ready**

Paper 1, Question 3

Question 3 in Paper 1 tests your ability to explain how the writer has used structure to affect the reader.

② Assessment objective 2

This question assesses AO2. For this you need to:
- explain, comment on and analyse how writers use structure to achieve effects and influence readers
- use relevant subject terminology.

To revise structural features and their correct subject terminology, go to pages 17–20.

② Structure

Structure is the way in which the writer organises their writing. To analyse structure you need to think about the shape of the text as a whole and the journey it takes the reader on.

⑤ Exam explainer

The question will tell you whether the source is taken from the beginning, middle or end of the text. Bear this in mind when you are analysing its structure.

3 You now need to think about the **whole** of the Source.

This text is from the opening of a novel.

How has the writer structured the text to interest you as a reader?

You could write about:

- what the writer focuses your attention on at the beginning
- how and why the writer changes this focus as the Source develops
- any other structural features that interest you.

[8 marks]

For this question you need to consider the whole of the source.

The command word is 'how'. This means you should write about what the writer has done, why they have done it and how it affects the reader.

Use the bullet points to help you structure your response.

It can be helpful to work through the text chronologically (from beginning to end) when answering this question.

② Checklist

Think about the whole text, including:
- ☑ the beginning
- ☑ the ending
- ☑ perspective shifts
- ☑ topic changes
- ☑ cohesion between paragraphs.

In your answer you will need to:
- ☑ select examples or features of structure
- ☑ analyse their effects
- ☑ use subject terminology.

② Exam focus

You should spend 60 minutes in total on Section A. Plan to spend 10 minutes on Question 3.

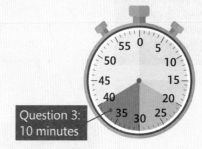

Question 3: 10 minutes

Pages
22–28
LINKS

Paper 1, Question 4

Question 4 in Paper 1 requires you to evaluate how successfully the writer has created an effect. You will need to bring together all your ideas on language and structure, and make a personal judgement.

Assessment objective 4

This question assesses AO4. For this you need to:

- evaluate a text critically
- support your evaluation with appropriate textual references.

You will need to analyse the language and structure of the source to support your ideas, so AO2 is covered in this question too. Question 4 brings together all the analysis skills you will have practised in Questions 2 and 3.

Evaluation

Evaluation means making an informed personal judgement about how effective the writer's choices are, and how successfully they achieve the writer's intention.

Go to pages 22–27 to revise evaluation.

Exam focus

You should spend 60 minutes in total on Section A.

Plan to spend 20 minutes on Question 4.

Question 4: 20 minutes

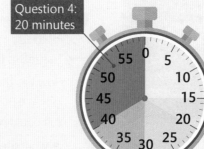

Checklist

☑ Think about whether you agree or disagree with the statement given in the question, and why.

☑ Choose examples that support your answer. You can include quotations and paraphrase longer sections.

☑ Consider the effect these have on the reader. Does it support the statement or not?

Exam explainer

Base your answer on the statement. It will always comment on what the writer has tried to achieve and how this affects the reader.

④ Focus this part of your answer on the second part of the Source from **line 17 to the end**.

Only use this section of the source in your answer.

A student, having read this section of the text, said: "The writer makes the relationship between the narrator and her parents very believable. I felt like I was 10 years old again."

To what extent do you agree?

First, decide how far you agree with the statement.

In your response, you could:

Use your personal response – how you felt and what you thought as you read the text – to inform your answer.

- write about your own impressions of the relationship between the narrator and her parents
- evaluate how the writer has created these impressions
- support your opinions with references to the text.

[20 marks]

Use quotations or paraphrasing as evidence for all of your points.

Analyse what choices the writer has made, why they made these choices and how effective they are.

Paper 1, Question 5

Question 5 in Paper 1 gives you a choice of two extended fiction writing tasks. It tests your ability to communicate clearly, structure your writing effectively and write with technical accuracy.

② Assessment objectives

AO5

This question tests AO5. For this you need to:

- communicate clearly, effectively and imaginatively, selecting and adapting tone, style and register for different forms, purposes and audiences
- organise information and ideas, using structural and grammatical features to support coherence and cohesion of text.

AO6

It also assesses AO6, your technical accuracy. For this you need to:

- use a range of vocabulary
- use a range of sentence structures
- spell accurately
- punctuate accurately.

Save a few minutes at the end to check your work.

See page 86 for advice on proofreading.

② Fiction writing

For this question you will write a piece of fiction on a similar theme to the source in Section A. You will need to use language and structure effectively to have an impact on a particular audience.

② Exam focus

You should spend 45 minutes in total on Section B.

Split this into 5 minutes planning, 35 minutes writing and 5 minutes proofreading.

Reading and planning: 5 minutes

Proofreading: 5 minutes

Question 5: 35 minutes

⑤ Exam explainer

5 You are going to enter a creative writing competition.

Your entry will be judged by a panel of people of your own age.

Either: Write a description suggested by this picture:

Or: Write the opening part of a story about visiting an exciting place.

(24 marks for content and organisation
16 marks for technical accuracy)

[40 marks]

You will always be given a specific audience and purpose.

One of the options will be based on an image.

You may be given a choice of two narrative writing tasks, two descriptive writing tasks or one narrative and one descriptive writing task.

Question 5 is worth 40 marks, split into 24 marks for content and organisation (AO5) and 16 marks for technical accuracy (AO6).

Paper 2, Question 1

Pages **29–32** LINKS

The first question in Paper 2 requires you to identify explicit and implicit information in the source.

② Reading time ✓

You should start Paper 2 by spending 15 minutes preparing. You should:

1 read the questions and underline the key words to find out what you need to look for in the sources

2 skim read the sources to identify the main ideas

3 read the sources again in more detail, annotating features you could use in your answers.

Go to page 31 to revise skimming.

② Assessment objective 1 ✓

This question assesses the first part of AO1. You will need to:

- identify and interpret explicit and implicit information and ideas.

You will need to use inference to find the implicit information in the source.

Go to page 7 to revise inference.

② Exam focus ✓

You should spend 60 minutes in total on Section A.
Plan to spend 5 minutes on Question 1.

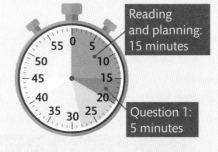

Reading and planning: 15 minutes

Question 1: 5 minutes

⑤ Exam explainer ✓

The command word is 'choose'. This means you should pick four options.

The question will tell you how many true statements you need to find.

Work through the statements one by one, making a small tick or cross against each.

6 Read again the first part of **Source A** from **lines 1 to 15**.

Choose **four** statements below which are TRUE.

- Shade the boxes of the ones that you think are true.
- Choose a maximum of four statements.

[4 marks]

A   The writer thinks short holidays are best. ◯

B   Travel involves visiting many other cultures. ◯

C   The writer believes in travelling in his own country. ◯

D   The writer always hitchhikes to exotic locations. ◯

E   The writer believes there are exotic locations in Britain. ◯

F   Every year the writer flies from Luton Airport. ◯

G   The writer's children refused to stay in a hostel. ◯

H   The writer is happy to get outside his comfort zone. ◯

The question will tell you which lines of the source to look at. Make sure you only use the given part of the text to answer this question.

The true statements will contain a mixture of implicit and explicit information from the source.

When you are happy with your answers, shade in the appropriate boxes.

 Made a start   **Feeling confident**   **Exam ready**

Paper 2, Question 2

For Question 2 in Paper 2 you will need to summarise the similarities or differences between two texts.

 Assessment objective 1

This question assesses the second part of AO1. You will need to:

- select and synthesise evidence from different texts.

You can use both explicit and implicit information. Use quotes and paraphrasing to give evidence from the sources.

 Synthesis

To synthesise means to bring together information from two or more texts. In this question, you do not need to analyse the language or structure of the sources.

To revise synthesis go to page 33.

 Exam explainer

2 You need to refer to **Source A** and **Source B** for this question.

Use details from **both** Sources. Write a summary of the differences between the journeys described by the writers.

[8 marks]

The command phrase is 'write a summary'. This means you should give an overview of the most important similarities or differences.

You should write about both sources in this question.

The question will ask you about either the similarities or the differences between the sources. Here, the question asks about the differences.

The question will ask you about a particular element in the sources. Focus your answer on this.

 Checklist

- ✓ Think about the connections between the two sources.
- ✓ Find the details in the sources that are relevant.
- ✓ Consider your own impression of these details (make inferences).
- ✓ Bring the two sets of details and inferences together in your answer.

 Exam focus

You should spend 60 minutes in total on Section A. Plan to spend 8 minutes on Question 2.

Question 2: 8 minutes

Paper 2, Question 3

Pages
36–39
LINKS

Question 3 in Paper 2 will test your ability to explain how writers use language to achieve effects in non-fiction writing.

 Assessment objective 2

This question assesses AO2. You will need to:

- explain, comment on and analyse how writers use language to achieve effects and influence readers
- use relevant subject terminology.

> To revise language features and their correct subject terminology, go to pages 36–38.

 Language

This question builds on the language analysis in Paper 1, Question 2. This time you have more freedom in your answer.

It does not give you a particular section to focus on, so you must choose examples from the text for yourself.

Similarly, it does not give bullet points to help you. However, you should still think about:

- words and phrases
- language features and techniques
- sentence forms.

 Exam explainer

> **3** You need to refer **only** to **Source B**, Robert Southey's article about visiting Birmingham.
>
> How does the writer use language to try to influence the reader?
> **[12 marks]**

The command word is 'how'. This means you should write about the language choices the writer has made, why they have done this and how it affects the reader.

You only need to focus on one of the texts for this question.

Focus your answer on the ways in which the writer tries to influence the reader.

 Exam focus

You can write about language techniques that are often used in fiction writing as well. Typical features that are in both fiction and non-fiction include:

- simile
- metaphor
- repetition
- direct address.

 Exam focus

You should spend 60 minutes in total on Section A. Plan to spend 12 minutes on Question 3.

Question 3: 12 minutes

✓ **Made a start** ✓ **Feeling confident** ✓ **Exam ready**

Paper 2, Question 4

For Question 4 in Paper 2 you will need to compare two non-fiction texts in detail.

 ## Assessment objective 3

This question assesses AO3. You will need to:

- compare writers' ideas and perspectives, as well as how these are conveyed, across two texts.

You will need to analyse the language and structure of the sources to support your ideas, so this question also tests AO1 and AO2. It brings together all the skills you have practised in the rest of the paper.

 ## Comparison

To compare the sources, you need to look for similarities or differences between them. You should think about what ideas the writers present, and also how they present them to influence the reader.

Go to pages 40–45 to revise comparison.

 ## Exam explainer

The command word is 'compare'. This means you should identify similarities and/ or differences between the texts.

Use the bullet points to help you structure your answer. However, you can add your own ideas too.

4 For this question, you need to refer to the **whole of Source A**, together with **Source B.**

Compare how the two writers convey their different attitudes to living in poverty.

In your answer, you could:

- compare their different attitudes
- compare the methods they use to convey their attitudes
- support your ideas with references to both texts.

[16 marks]

You should consider both sources equally.

The question will focus on the writers' points of view on a particular topic. Make sure your answer sticks to this focus.

'Methods' means the form, structure and language used by the writers to influence the reader.

 ## Exam focus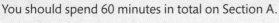

You should spend 60 minutes in total on Section A.

Plan to spend 20 minutes on Question 4.

This is the most complex question in Paper 2, so it is important to think about how you will structure your answer.

Spend 5 minutes planning and 15 minutes writing.

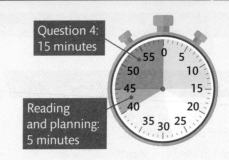

Question 4: 15 minutes

Reading and planning: 5 minutes

Paper 2, Question 5

Pages 61–76
LINKS

Question 5 in Paper 2 will test your ability to present a viewpoint. You will need to show that you can write non-fiction for different audiences and purposes.

② Assessment objectives

AO5

This question tests AO5. For this you need to:

- communicate clearly, effectively and imaginatively, selecting and adapting tone, style and register for different forms, purposes and audiences
- organise information and ideas, using structural and grammatical features to support coherence and cohesion of text.

AO6

It also assesses AO6, your technical accuracy. For this you need to:

- use a range of vocabulary
- use a range of sentence structures
- spell accurately
- punctuate accurately.

② Presenting your viewpoint

For this writing question, you will need to present your own point of view on a topic in response to a statement. You will need to use form, language and structure carefully to have an impact on a particular audience.

The purpose of your writing will be to present your opinion. This will involve a combination of explaining, arguing, informing and persuading.

② Form

The question will tell you what form to write in. It could be:

- a speech
- an essay
- a letter
- a leaflet.
- an article

⑤ Exam explainer

5 'Reality TV is full of ageing has-beens and talentless people desperate to be famous. It is a waste of our time.'

Write an article for a broadsheet newspaper in which you explain your point of view on this statement.

(24 marks for content and organisation

16 marks for technical accuracy)

[40 marks]

Your purpose will always be to present your point of view.

In Paper 2 you will not have a choice of writing tasks.

You will be given a statement linked to the texts you have read to inspire your writing.

You will be told what form to write in. You might also be told who the audience is, or you may have to infer it from the form. An article for a broadsheet newspaper suggests an adult audience.

There are 40 marks available, split into 24 marks for content and organisation (AO5) and 16 marks for technical accuracy (AO6).

② Checklist

Save a few minutes at the end to check your work. Ask yourself these questions:

- ✓ Have I missed any words?
- ✓ Have I used punctuation correctly?
- ✓ Have I spelled everything accurately?

See page 86 for advice on proofreading.

② Exam focus

You should spend 45 minutes on Section B.

Split this into 5 minutes planning, 35 minutes writing and 5 minutes proofreading.

Reading and planning: 5 minutes

Question 5: 35 minutes

Proofreading: 5 minutes

✓ **Made a start** ✓ **Feeling confident** ✓ **Exam ready**

Types of fiction text

Paper 1, Section A contains four questions about **one** extract taken from either a 20th-century or a 21st-century work of fiction.

② Fiction

Fiction is writing that comes from the writer's imagination. It can be based on history or fact, but it doesn't need to be true. Fiction texts are always creative and use language techniques to create meaning and interest for the reader.

Prose is the ordinary form of written language that you would usually find in a novel.

② Genre

Genre is the name given to a style or category of literature. The source in Section A could be from any fiction genre, including:

- science fiction
- historical
- romance
- dystopian
- detective
- realism
- thriller
- crime.

A dystopia is an imagined society where life is unpleasant or bad in some way. 'The Handmaid's Tale' by Margaret Atwood is an example of a dystopian novel.

② Exam focus

The source in Paper 1, Section A will be an extract from a longer story. It will be taken from a key point, such as the beginning, a turning point or the end.

Read the information about the source carefully to find out where in the story it is from, and bear this in mind when you answer the questions.

② The protagonist

The **protagonist** is the main character in a story and will often undergo some kind of change or development during the course of the story. They do not have to be good or likeable, although in many cases they will be.

An **antagonist** is a character who is in opposition to the protagonist, such as an adversary or enemy.

⑤ Forms of fiction

The source in Paper 1 is likely to be an extract from a short story, novella or novel.

Short stories

Short stories can be up to a few thousand words long, and may be intended to be read in a single sitting. Common features include:

- a focus on creating an atmosphere or exploring an idea, rather than telling a detailed story
- one or two characters
- a surprising or sudden ending, such as a cliffhanger or twist.

Novels

Novels are longer stories and can be anything from a few hundred to several thousand pages long. Common features include:

- a number of interlinked plot lines
- a greater number of characters
- chapters.

Many novels tell the whole story of a **protagonist's** life.

Novellas

Novellas are longer than short stories but shorter than full novels. Common features include:

- a single plot line
- a small number of characters
- one or two locations.

② Themes

Works of fiction are often based on **themes**. A theme is a recurring idea that is central to the narrative. Common themes include love, friendship, memory and revenge.

⑩ Practice

Spend at least ten minutes each day reading fiction. Aim to read from a wide variety of genres and forms.

See how many main themes you can identify in each text you read.

Explicit information

Paper 1, Question 1 will test your ability to identify and retrieve explicit information from the source text.

② Explicit information

Explicit information is stated clearly, leaving no room for confusion or doubt. If information is explicit, its meaning is obvious and generally straightforward to understand.

In Paper 1, Question 1:

- you do not need to look for hidden meanings
- you do not have to explain the information you find
- you can give short quotations or paraphrase the information.

① Exam focus

Read the question carefully and underline the key words to help you identify the focus. In the example below, the question is about the houses on the street, not the street itself.

② Paper 1, Question 1

You will always be asked to identify four things. You won't get extra marks for more than this.

The question will tell you which lines to look at in the source. Only write about information from this section.

> 1. Read again the first part of the Source from **lines 4 to 8**.
>   List **four** things from this part of the text about the <u>character's appearance</u>.
>
> **[4 marks]**

The question will focus on a single element of the text.

There is one mark available for each point you make.

⑩ Worked example

Source – The Cuckoo's Calling

This is the opening of a detective novel. In this section, the narrator describes the media waiting outside a crime scene.

To fill the time, the woolly-hatted cameramen filmed the backs of the photographers, the balcony, the tent concealing the body, then repositioned themselves for wide shots that encompassed the chaos that had exploded inside the sedate and snowy Mayfair street, with its lines of glossy black doors framed by white stone porticos[1] and flanked by topiary shrubs. The entrance to number 18 was bounded with tape. Police officials, some of them white-clothed forensic experts, could be glimpsed in the hallway beyond.

Glossary:

porticos[1] – porches

Read again this extract from **lines 1 to 5** of the Source.

List **four** things from this part of the text about the houses on the street. **[4 marks]**

1 They have 'glossy black doors'.

2 They have 'white stone porticos'.

3 They have shrubs outside.

4 One has police tape outside.

In quotations, use the exact words in the source, copy them correctly and use quotation marks.

In paraphrasing, be as clear and concise as possible.

⑤ Exam-style practice

Read again this extract from **lines 1 to 3** of the Source.

List **four** things from this part of the text about what is happening on the street.

Source – The Cuckoo's Calling

Behind the tightly packed paparazzi stood white vans with enormous satellite dishes on the roofs, and journalists talking, some in foreign languages, while soundmen in headphones hovered. Between recordings, the reporters stamped their feet and warmed their hands on hot beakers of coffee from the teeming café a few streets away.

Paper 1, Question 1

This question assesses your ability to identify explicit information and ideas. To 'identify', you should find the relevant information in the source and quote or paraphrase it in your answer. Look at the worked examples and then try the exam-style practice.

 Worked example

> **Source B, lines 7–10**
>
> The train jolts and scrapes and screeches back into motion, the little pile of clothes disappears from view and we trundle on towards London, moving at a brisk jogger's pace. Someone in the seat behind me gives a sigh of helpless irritation; the 8:04 slow train from Ashbury to Euston can test the patience of the most seasoned commuter.

Read again this extract from Source B on page 92 from **lines 7 to 10**.

List **four** things from this part of the text about the train. **[4 marks]**

1 The train is going to London.

2 It moves at a 'brisk jogger's pace'.

3 It is a slow train.

4 It leaves Ashbury at 8.04.

> Focus on explicit information only. You do not need to infer anything.

> Use short, precise paraphrasing.

 Worked example

> **Source – Paddy Clarke Ha Ha Ha**
>
> We were flinging water at each other. We'd stopped laughing cos we'd been doing it for ages. The tide was going out so we'd be getting out in a minute. Edward Swanwick pushed his hands out and sent a wave towards me and there was a jellyfish in it. A huge see-through one with pink veins and a purple middle. I lifted my arms way up and started to move but it still rubbed my side. I screamed. I pushed through the water to the steps. I felt the jellyfish hit my back; I thought I did. I yelled again; I couldn't help it. It was rocky and uneven down at the seafront, not like the beach. I got to the steps and grabbed the bar.

Read again this extract from **lines 1 to 6** of the Source.

List **four** things from this part of the text about the sea. **[4 marks]**

1 The tide was going out.

2 There were steps down to the sea.

3 The narrator and Edward Swanwick were in the sea.

4 There was a jellyfish in the sea.

> Make four clear, separate points.

> Only use explicit information.

> Use a mixture of quotation and paraphrasing if you prefer.

 Exam focus

In Paper 1, Question 1:

- you don't have to write your answers in full sentences
- you don't need to interpret your answers in any way
- there will be more than four pieces of information in the section of text – choose the four that you can quote or paraphrase most concisely.

 Exam-style practice

Read again Source B on page 92 from **lines 18 to 20**.

List **four** things from this part of the text about what is happening on the train.

[4 marks]

 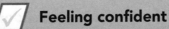

Critical analysis

Taking a critical approach will help you to formulate a strong response to Paper 1, Question 2. It will also help you with other analysis questions in Paper 1.

What, how and why

Your critical analysis needs to be detailed and carefully structured. For every point you make, answer these three questions.

1 **What** has the writer done? Identify a key effect they have created or a choice they have made: *The writer creates an exciting atmosphere.*

2 **How** have they done it? Give an example (either a quotation or paraphrase) and analyse it: *The list of energetic verbs, 'running, leaping, sprinting', creates a fast pace.*

3 **Why** have they done it? Explain the effect it has on the reader: *This makes the reader feel as though they are in the middle of the action, rushing along with the narrator.*

Critical questions

Every time you read a piece of fiction, think about these questions.

- ☑ What is the first thing you find out about the plot or the characters in the opening?
- ☑ Is the ending happy, sad or a cliffhanger?
- ☑ What is the narrative perspective? Who is telling the story?
- ☑ How is the setting described?
- ☑ Is the atmosphere happy, frightening or comic?
- ☑ What do you learn about the characters?
- ☑ How do you feel about the characters?

Then, for each point, ask yourself: **how** has the writer achieved this, and **why** did they choose to do it?

Worked example

Source – Empire of the Sun

This is an extract from a novel set in Singapore during the First World War. In this section, a boy's mother has been taken away by soldiers.

His mother's clothes were scattered across the unmade bed, and open suitcases lay on the floor. Someone had swept her hairbrushes and scent bottles from the dressing table, and talcum covered the polished parquet. There were dozens of footprints in the powder, his mother's bare feet whirling within the clear images of heavy boots, like the patterns of complicated dances set out in his parents' foxtrot and tango manuals.

Look in detail at this extract from **lines 1 to 4** of the Source.

How does the writer use language here to describe his mother's room? **[8 marks]**

The writer uses language to create a sense of violence. For example, the verb 'scattered' and the adjective 'unmade' suggest that the mother left in a hurry, while the verb 'swept' suggests the soldiers were destructive. Overall, the language used to describe the room clearly shows that the soldiers were forceful...

In addition, this is a really detailed visual description. We are shown the mother's bare footprints contrasted with the soldiers' 'heavy boots'. The fact that the mother's feet are bare makes her seem weak compared with the soldiers, leading the reader to feel she can't protect herself against them...

Identify **what** the writer has done. It could be an effect they have created or a significant choice they have made.

Explain **how** they have done it. Quote or paraphrase an example, and then explain how it achieves the effect you identified. Use technical terms such as 'verb' and 'adjective' to form a clear explanation.

Use the information about the source to help you fully understand it.

Suggest **why** the writer has done it. Focus on how it affects the reader. You could develop your answer by thinking about whether the effect is intended.

Practice

Read Source C on page 93. Use the what, how and why structure to write a paragraph about the source's opening.

☑ **Made a start** ☑ **Feeling confident** ☑ **Exam ready**

Word classes

You should use accurate subject terminology when you comment on the writer's language choices. Make sure you can comment in detail on nouns, adjectives, verbs and adverbs.

 Word class examples

Common nouns refer to things, such as 'kites, 'sky' and 'hour'.

Proper nouns are the names of people and places, such as 'Hassan' and 'Afghanistan'. They always have capital letters.

Abstract nouns refer to feelings and ideas, such as 'triumph' and 'happiness'.

Adverbial phrases such as 'up and down the streets' are phrases that work in the same way as adverbs.

Adverbs, such as 'triumphantly' and 'carefully', are a type of **modifier** used to describe verbs.

Source D, lines 1 to 19

This extract is from the middle of a novel by Khaled Hosseini, set in Afghanistan in 1975. In this section, a boy and his friend Hassan are taking part in a kite fighting competition.

At least two dozen <u>kites</u> already hung <u>in</u> the <u>sky</u>, like paper sharks roaming for prey. Within an <u>hour</u>, the number doubled, and red, blue, and <u>yellow</u> kites <u>glided</u> and <u>spun</u> in the sky. A <u>cold</u> breeze <u>wafted</u> through my hair. The wind <u>was</u> <u>perfect</u> for kite flying, blowing just hard enough to give some lift, make the sweeps easier. Next to me, <u>Hassan</u> held the spool, his hands already bloodied by the string [...]

<u>Up and down the streets</u>, kite runners were returning <u>triumphantly</u>, their captured kites held high. They showed them off to their parents, their friends. But they all knew the <u>best</u> was yet to come. The <u>biggest</u> prize of all was still flying. I sliced a bright yellow kite with a coiled white tail.

Prepositions such as 'in', 'after' and 'through' tell you about the relationship between words or phrases within a sentence.

Verbs, such as 'wafted', 'glided' and 'spun', express actions. Verbs such as 'to be' express states, for example: 'the wind <u>was</u> perfect'.

Adjectives, such as 'yellow', 'cold' and 'perfect', are a type of **modifier** used to describe nouns.

Comparative and **superlative** adjectives are used to compare nouns. Comparatives include 'bigger', 'hotter' and 'better'. Superlatives include 'biggest' and 'best'.

  Pronouns

Pronouns are words that replace other nouns:
- personal pronouns – 'I', 'me', 'you', 'us', 'he'
- possessive pronouns – 'mine', 'yours', 'ours', 'theirs'
- demonstrative pronouns – 'that', 'this', 'those'
- indefinite pronouns – 'some', 'any', 'everyone'.

Writers use pronouns to avoid repetition and improve **cohesion**. Go to page 19 to revise cohesion.

  Aiming higher

It can sometimes be useful to identify which word classes the writer has or has not used and why.

For example, the writer of Source D uses a number of adjectives, such as 'red, blue and yellow... bright yellow... coiled white' to create a vivid visual impression of the kites in the sky.

 Verbs

Carefully chosen verbs can add detail to a text. In the extract from Source D, the verb 'roaming' suggests that the kites are predatory, while the verbs 'gliding' and 'spinning' suggest that they are also elegant.

Imperative verbs are used to give commands, for example: 'Run!' This often creates a sense of authority or urgency.

Modal verbs such as 'can', 'should' and 'must' express ability, obligation or necessity.

  **Modifiers**

Modifiers add descriptive detail, which helps the reader imagine the scene more clearly. In the extract from Source D, for example, the adjective 'cold' before 'breeze' suggests the refreshing feeling of the wind.

Adverbs can also provide information about time and place. For instance, 'already' is an adverb of time and 'here' is an adverb of place.

In some cases, adverbs can modify adjectives or other adverbs, for example: 'horribly cold' or 'really slowly'.

  Practice

Write a paragraph about each of these words, identifying its word class and explaining its effect in the extract above.
a) captured
b) triumphantly

 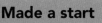 **Made a start** 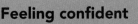 **Feeling confident** **Exam ready**

Words and phrases

For both papers, you need to be able to identify what vocabulary choices a writer has made, suggest why they made these choices and explain how they might affect the reader.

 Word choices

Every word or phrase in a text has been deliberately chosen by the writer to create a particular effect. Look for significant words and think about how they shape the reader's picture of the scene.

The General laughed loudly and bellowed, 'Drop and give me twenty!'

In this example, the writer uses unpleasant language to describe the General. The verb 'bellowed' suggests that he is loud and aggressive while the phrase 'laughed loudly' implies that he is enjoying his power. This might make the reader imagine that he is frightening and cruel.

You should also aim to analyse the **connotations** of the writer's word choices. Go to page 8 to revise connotations.

 Aiming higher

Patterns in a writer's language choices can reveal themes and deeper meanings. Patterns can be created in several ways.

1 **Repetition** of words or phrases, for example: **It's all work, work, work.** Or repetition of certain types of word, for example: **The butterfly leapt, swirled and twirled.**

2 Use of words from the same **semantic field**. A semantic field is a group of words that can be linked together under the same theme. For example, **He drank in the air and relished the roasting heat of the day** uses the semantic field of food.

 Worked example

Look in detail at **lines 18 to 23** of Source B on page 92. How does the writer use language here to describe the train journey?

[8 marks]

> Use subject terminology to accurately discuss language choices.

The writer uses onomatopoeia to describe what it is like to be inside the train. The onomatopoeic word 'jingles' sounds startling and therefore annoying for the narrator. Similarly, 'rustle' and 'tap' capture the irritating sounds of the other passengers fidgeting. The writer uses the verb 'feel' rather than 'hear' in this sentence, which makes the narrator seem even more intensely aware of the annoying sounds...

The writer chooses clumsy verbs such as 'lurches and sways' to describe how the train moves. These choices make the train sound not just slow, but also unsteady, highlighting how uncomfortable the journey is for the narrator. The use of the synonyms 'lurch' and 'sway' together creates a repetitive effect, and the writer also uses repetition in other phrases, such as 'on and on' and 'I try not to look up, I try to read'. This makes the journey seem frustrating and tedious...

 Patterns in sound

Writers sometimes choose words because of the sounds they create when said aloud. This could emphasise key information or involve the reader's hearing in a description to make them feel as though they are really there.

Alliteration is repetition of a letter at the start of two or more words. In this example, the hard 't' sounds reflect the tree's size and strength: **The tall tree towered overhead.**

Sibilance is repetition of the letter 's', for example: **I silently slipped around the corner.** This could sound soft and gentle, or sneaky and snake-like.

Assonance is repetition of a vowel sound. Here, the rounded vowels suggest a booming, echoing sound: **The sound bounced around the crowds.**

Onomatopoeia is when a writer uses a word to mimic a noise. For example, in the description **intercoms crackled**, the word 'crackled' captures the actual sound made.

> Explain **what** the writer has done, **how** they have done it, and **why** they have done it.

> Think about how the writer has used sound to emphasise information or add extra sensory detail to a description.

> Look for patterns such as repetition in the writer's word choices.

 Exam-style practice

Look in detail at **lines 1 to 6** of Source B on page 92. How does the writer use language here to describe the view?

   Made a start 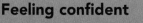 **Feeling confident** **Exam ready**

Inference

Writers often suggest information for the reader to infer. Inference is an important skill in English, which you will need to use in many of the questions in your exam.

② Inference

There is more to fiction than the literal meaning of the words. Writers can suggest additional meaning through patterns, themes, language choices or even what they leave unsaid. Inference is reading between the lines to work out things which are not explicitly stated in a text.

② Prompt questions

- ☑ What is my impression after reading the text?
- ☑ What clues has the writer provided?
- ☑ Does my idea fit with the text as a whole?
- ☑ Can I provide evidence to support my impression?

⑩ Worked example

Look in detail at **lines 12 to 20** of Source E on page 95. How does the writer use language here to describe the family home?

You could include the writer's choice of:

- words and phrases
- language features and techniques
- sentence forms.

[8 marks]

The garden is described as 'wild' and 'overgrown', and the pond is 'scummy' which implies that no one has bothered to do any gardening for a long time. Similarly, the 'scurry of small lives' suggests that animals have taken over because people do not go out there very often. The reader might feel sorry for Rahel seeing her family garden in such an abandoned state...

However, the car outside is described in flashy language as a 'skyblue Plymouth' with shiny 'chrome tailfins'. This implies that the car is looked after much better than anything else in the scene. The contrast might make the reader feel angry that whoever lives there can care so much about the car, but so little about the house...

Identify **what** the author has done. Then, explain **how** they have done it by analysing an example. Finally, suggest **why** they have done it, focusing on what additional meanings the reader might infer.

Support your inference with short, relevant evidence.

Use phrases such as 'this implies' to explain your ideas and show you are using inference.

Explain your thought process as clearly as possible.

② Writing about inference

Use phrases such as 'this suggests' and 'this implies' to explain clearly how you have inferred information from the text.

You can also use tentative language such as 'might', 'maybe' and 'perhaps' to show that you are reading between the lines.

⑩ Practice

Read Source B on page 92.

Explain three things that you can infer about the narrator.

Connotations

Some words suggest ideas or associations beyond their literal meaning. These linked ideas or feelings are called connotations.

 Exploring connotations

Writers choose their words very carefully to suggest extra layers of meaning. The reader can then infer more detail by thinking about the connotations of the writer's word choices. A writer may use several words with similar connotations to create a particularly strong impression. For example, the words 'snow... winter... cold... freezing... numbing... biting...' build an impression of discomfort and danger. Most words have more than one connotation, so you need to look at the context in which the word is used. Look at the spider diagram for more possible connotations of the word 'snow'.

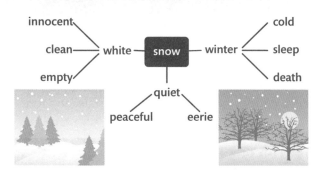

 Worked example

> **Source – The Cuckoo's Calling**
>
> *This is the opening of a detective novel. In this section, reporters are waiting outside a crime scene.*
>
> The buzz in the street was like the humming of flies. Photographers stood massed behind barriers patrolled by police, their long-snouted cameras poised, their breath rising like steam. Snow fell steadily on to hats and shoulders; gloved fingers wiped lenses clear...
>
> To fill the time, the woolly-hatted cameramen filmed the backs of the photographers, the balcony, the tent concealing the body, then repositioned themselves for wide shots that encompassed the chaos that had exploded inside the sedate and snowy Mayfair street, with its lines of glossy black doors framed by white stone porticos and flanked by topiary shrubs. The entrance to number 18 was bounded with tape.

Look in detail at this extract from **lines 1 to 7** of the Source. How does the writer use language here to describe the reporters? You could include the writer's choice of:

- words and phrases
- language features and techniques
- sentence forms.

[8 marks]

The writer describes the photographers' cameras as 'long-snouted'. This description links the photographers with pigs, which have connotations of greediness and dirtiness. It suggests that they are behaving like animals.

In addition, the nouns 'humming' and 'buzz' are used to describe the noise the reporters are making. When combined with the noun 'flies' this has connotations of dirt and disease.

Altogether, these connotations paint an image of animals feeding on something disgusting...

> Look for multiple words or phrases that have similar connotations. Think about whether these create a deliberate effect.

> Consider the context carefully. This will affect a word's connotations.

> Look for patterns of connotations that work together to create a combined effect.

 Aiming higher

A word may have several very different connotations. Writers can use these to create contrasting impressions in the reader's mind. For example, a snowy mountain may seem quiet and peaceful but also cold, silent and dangerous.

 Practice

1. Make a mind map exploring the connotations of each of these words from the extract.
   a) glossy   b) exploded   c) sedate

2. Write a paragraph analysing the overall effect the writer has created by using these words in their description of the street.

 Made a start **Feeling confident** **Exam ready**

Figurative language

Figurative language is where a writer uses language in a non-literal way to create a particular effect in the mind of the reader. Metaphors and similes are examples of figurative language devices.

Similes

A **simile** is where a writer directly compares one thing to another in order to create a particularly clear image in the reader's mind. This is usually done using 'like' or 'as'. This example suggests a harsh voice, perhaps saying something hurtful: **Her voice was as sharp as a knife.**

Similes can sometimes be formed as compound adjectives: **He had cat-like balance.**

Metaphors

A **metaphor** is another way to compare two different things. Rather than using 'like' or 'as', a metaphor says something **is** something else. For example, the metaphor **My phone is a dinosaur** creates a comic description of a slow, outdated mobile phone that is out of place in the modern world.

An **extended metaphor** is when a comparison is developed in different ways over a sentence, a paragraph or even longer, for example: **My phone is a dinosaur: slow, huge and heavy, and soon to be extinct.**

Worked example

Look in detail at **lines 1 to 9** of Source A on page 91. How does the writer use language here to describe the scene on the street?

You could include the writer's choice of:

- words and phrases
- language features and techniques
- sentence forms.   **[8 marks]**

The writer uses language to create a scene that seems dangerous and tense by using the simile 'vice-like'. A 'vice' is a tool that grips very tightly, suggesting that the cold is closing in on the people in the street. It is a threatening image, because a vice could be used to inflict torture and pain. This gives the scene a feeling of danger.

The writer develops this sense of danger by describing the pipe as having a 'fat lip'. This personification creates a disturbing image of the pipe as a person who has been in a fight. In addition, the water that 'drips' from it suggests blood, perhaps foreshadowing a violent event. Furthermore, the trees are described using the metaphor 'bleached bone-white'. The imagery of skeletons again suggests danger and death, making the reader feel tense...

Personification

Sometimes writers describe something non-human as if it is alive and has human qualities. This is called **personification**. For example, in the sentence **The flowers danced in the breeze**, the writer has attributed the human action of dancing to the flowers to describe how they move around attractively in the wind.

Pathetic fallacy is a kind of personification that gives human emotions to non-human objects in nature. It is commonly used to reflect a character's emotions through the weather, for example: **The grey clouds frowned and groaned overhead as Jo fell deeper into depression.** Here, the clouds are personified to echo the character's gloomy, stormy feelings.

> Use the correct subject terminology.

> Use the **what, how, why** structure to talk about each of your points in detail. Go to page 4 to revise this structure.

> Make links between language choices with similar effects.

Practice

Look in detail at this extract from **lines 1 to 2** of the Source. How does the writer use language features and techniques here to describe the river?

Source – The God of Small Things

A thin ribbon of thick water [...] lapped wearily at the mud banks on either side, sequinned with the occasional silver slant of a dead fish. It was choked with a succulent weed, whose furred brown roots waved like thin tentacles underwater.

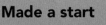 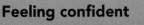

Sentence forms

The way in which a writer structures their sentences can have as much impact on a reader as their word choices. You should consider sentence forms in both papers.

⑤ **Types of clause**

Clauses are the building blocks of sentences. Every clause contains one piece of information and includes at least one subject and one verb. They can be linked together with conjunctions such as 'until', 'but', 'because' and 'so'.

- A **main clause** expresses a complete thought and can work as a sentence on its own.

- If there are two or more main clauses in a sentence, they are called **coordinate clauses**. They often create a sense of cause and effect: **Beth fell off her chair and Riley sniggered.** They can also describe several things happening at once: **The tyres screeched and the car spun.**

- **Subordinate clauses** do not express a complete thought on their own and depend on a main clause, for example: **He rushed outside <u>although it was raining</u>.** A subordinate clause can be placed at different points in a sentence to produce different effects. For example, the first of these sentences has more suspense than the second:
When I saw what was in the box, I gasped.
I gasped when I saw what was in the box.

  A conjunction that introduces a subordinate clause is a **subordinating conjunction**.

⑤ **Types of sentences**

- ☑ **Single-clause sentences** contain just one main clause and no subordinate clauses. Writers use short single-clause sentences to emphasise a key piece of information, for example: **There was no going back.** Using a string of these can create a slow or jerky pace, for example: **The light changed to green. We waited. Finally, the car inched forwards.**

- ☑ **Multi-clause sentences** are made up of two or more clauses joined together. One or more subordinate clauses can be added to a main clause to provide extra detail or information: **Pip, who is my best friend, was sitting behind me.**
  Several main and subordinate clauses can be combined to form a long multi-clause sentence. This might create a fast pace: **The wolf, who appeared from nowhere, growled and I leapt backwards as Ashish yelled and Tasha dropped the torch.**

- ☑ **Minor sentences** do not express a complete thought on their own, so are grammatically incomplete, for example: **Absolutely not.** Writers sometimes use them to add drama or emphasis.

⑩ **Worked example**

Look in detail at **lines 31 to 34** of Source A on page 91. How does the writer use language here to describe the old man's movements? **[8 marks]**

The writer uses a range of sentence forms to describe the old man's movements. For example, there are lots of single-clause sentences, such as 'The old man in the wheelchair appears.' These slow down the pace of the description and suggest how slowly and painfully he moves.

> When you identify a sentence form, make sure you explore the effect it has on the reader.

Even the fourth sentence, which is a long multi-clause sentence, ends with the words 'small push', drawing the reader's attention back to the old man's slow stopping and starting.

> Paraphrase longer sentences or refer to them by number.

The writer also uses very short minor sentences to describe the noises that the old man makes: 'Huh. Hah. Huh.' This draws attention to the effort that goes into each movement and suggests that he is breathless, encouraging the reader to sympathise with him...

> Look at each sentence in context. A short sentence might create tension in one context, but a peaceful pause in another.

⑩ **Practice**

Look in detail at **lines 1 to 11** of Source E on page 95.

How does the writer use sentence forms here to interest the reader?

Reading the question

You should read all the questions on the exam paper very carefully to make sure you know exactly what you need to do.

10 Worked example

Source – Gone Girl

When I think of my wife, I always think of her head. The shape of it, to begin with. The very first time I saw her, it was the back of the head I saw, and there was something lovely about it, the angles of it. Like a shiny, hard corn kernel or a riverbed fossil. She had what the Victorians would call *a finely shaped head*. You could imagine the skull quite easily.

I'd know her head anywhere.

And what's inside it. I think of that, too: her mind. Her brain, all those coils, and her thoughts shuttling through those coils like fast, frantic centipedes. Like a child, I picture opening her skull, unspooling her brain and sifting through it, trying to catch and pin down her thoughts.

Look in detail at this extract from **lines 1 to 7** of the Source.

How does the writer use <u>language</u> here to describe <u>the narrator's wife</u>?

You could include the writer's choice of:

- <u>words and phrases</u>
- <u>language features and techniques</u>
- <u>sentence forms.</u>

[8 marks]

The writer uses very negative language to describe his wife. In the opening of the extract the narrator describes the shape of his wife's head as a 'shiny, hard corn kernel' and a 'fossil'. This straight away creates an uncomfortable feeling because the similes seem harsh and insulting, suggesting the narrator does not like his wife...

The narrator continues to use unpleasant imagery throughout the extract. He describes his wife's thoughts as 'frantic centipedes' and imagines 'unspooling' her brain. The writer uses a long multi-clause sentence to match her 'fast, frantic' thoughts using language choices that suggest her thoughts are horrible and frightening. This builds on the description in the first paragraph, creating a very negative impression of the narrator's wife...

Make sure you clearly explain the effect that the writer's language has on the reader.

2 Reading questions

As you read each question, highlight or underline:

- the part of the source you need to look at
- the skill(s) you need to demonstrate
- the focus of the question.

2 Exam focus

Use the key words in the question to structure your answer. This will help you to stay focused on what the question is asking about.

If line numbers are given in the question, you should only write about that part of the source. If you are not given the extract as part of the question, mark in the margin of your source text which lines these are.

If a question asks 'how' a writer does something, it is asking you to write about the methods they have used and the effect these have on the reader.

Underline the key words in the question to identify its focus.

Some questions will include bullet points with ideas or reminders to help you. Try to include everything the question suggests in your answer.

Always use paraphrasing or short, carefully chosen quotations to back up your points.

Use key words from the question to keep your answer focused.

10 Practice

Underline the key words in this exam-style question.

Look in detail at this extract from **lines 1 to 8** of Source E on page 95.

How does the writer use language to describe the atmosphere at the house?

You could include the writer's choice of:

- words and phrases
- language forms and techniques
- sentence forms.

Annotating the text

Annotating the sources in your exams will help you to locate useful information easily and quickly.

(2) Annotation

To annotate, underline or highlight a significant feature in the text and make a short note about why it is important. In the exam, keep your annotations short and simple to save time. You do not need to write your notes in sentences.

(2) Exam focus

Before you start to annotate:
- read the question carefully
- check which lines you need to read
- underline the key words to identify the focus.

(2) Useful notes

Having clear, useful notes will help you to plan and write your answers more efficiently. For each feature you underline, make notes about:
- **what** the writer has done
- **how** they have done it
- **why** they have done it.

You then have everything you need to write up each note as a well-organised paragraph.

(2) Subject terminology

Use subject specific vocabulary in your annotations wherever possible. This will allow you to be more precise and will remind you to include the correct terms in your answer.

Remember, you don't need to stick to this order of what, how and why when you write your answer from these notes. Make your points as concisely as possible.

(10) Worked example

Look in detail at this extract from **lines 1 to 3** of the Source.

How does the writer use language here to describe the scene? **[8 marks]**

> **Source – Empire of the Sun**
>
> *This extract is set in China in the Second World War. In this section, a young boy is in a dock, looking at a big ship called the Idzumo.*
>
> Cold <u>sunlight shivered</u> on the river, turning its surface into <u>chopped glass,</u> and transforming the distant banks and hotels of the Bund into <u>a row of wedding cakes</u>. To Jim, as he sat on the catwalk of the funeral pier below the deserted Nantao shipyards, the funnels and masts of the *Idzumo* seemed <u>carved from icing sugar.</u>

What: personification. How: sun shivering. Why: unsettling, unnatural effect. Suggests danger.

What: metaphor. How: water = broken glass. Why: suggests danger and pain. Water not safe.

What: metaphor. How: buildings = wedding cakes. Why: connotations of white/wedding = pure, peace, love. Juxtaposition with danger.

> The personification of the sun in the phrase 'the sunlight shivered' creates an unnatural feeling because the sun seems cold, although it is usually associated with warmth. Its 'shiver' also appeals to the reader's senses by reminding them of a shiver running down their spine, which suggests that something unpleasant is about to happen. This makes the scene feel dangerous...

Use key words from your annotations to structure your answer.

Fully expand the ideas from your notes in your answer.

Make sure you explain how each feature affects the reader.

(5) Practice

1 Annotate the final underlined part of the Source in the worked example ('carved from icing sugar').

2 Use your annotations to write a further paragraph continuing the model answer in the worked example.

Made a start | Feeling confident | Exam ready

Using evidence

For both exam papers, you will need to use carefully chosen evidence from the sources to support each of your points.

② Embedding quotations

An embedded quotation forms part of your sentence. To embed a quotation you should:

☑ use the shortest possible quotation that supports your point

☑ use quotation marks

☑ check that the sentence and quotation make sense together

☑ check you have copied the quotation accurately.

② Paraphrasing

Paraphrasing is where you put part of a text into your own words without changing the writer's meaning. Use paraphrasing when:

☑ the part of the text you need to refer to is too long to quote

☑ you want to summarise something

☑ you need to refer to a structural technique that you can't quote.

② Working with long quotations

With some sources, there may be longer sections that you want to use as quotations, such as a few whole sentences. Instead of copying them out, it is better to paraphrase them or to embed the most important words.

You can also show where you have left words out of a long quotation with an ellipsis (...): 'The wound... went three floors deep.'

To choose the key parts of a quotation, think about the point you are making and the particular words and phrases that support it.

> Where possible, use short embedded quotations. This is quicker and helps you focus on specific choices the writer has made.

> Instead of using a long quotation, choose the key language you want to discuss. This answer paraphrases the underlined text and embeds specific words from it.

> Discuss the effect of your quotations in detail.

> Use paraphrasing to give evidence of more general choices that are difficult to quote directly and use ellipses to shorten some quotations.

⑩ Worked example

Look in detail at this extract from **lines 1 to 6** of the Source.

How does the writer use language here to describe the ruined hotel? **[8 marks]**

> **Source – High Dive**
>
> *In this section of the text, there has just been an explosion at a hotel.*
>
> The night sky had eaten into the roofline. <u>The wound in the building went three floors deep. Smoke gushed up out of the dark space where the rooms were supposed to live</u>. The railings of balconies arced down, trailing off into nothing. Rubble tumbled in from left and right.

The verb 'eaten' uses personification to create the impression that the explosion is like a dangerous and threatening predator. This impression continues with the description of the hotel. It is presented as though it has been injured by the predator, with smoke gushing like blood from its 'deep' 'wound', suggesting how badly damaged it is. Similarly, the description of rubble tumbling from all sides and 'railings... trailing off into nothing' creates a feeling of chaos and confusion...

② Exam focus

Choose quotations carefully. Make sure your evidence supports your point and enables you to explain your ideas.

⑩ Exam-style practice

Answer this exam-style question, using both quotations and paraphrasing to present your evidence.

> Look in detail at **lines 17 to 27** of Source A on page 91.
>
> How does the writer use language here to show time passing?

Structuring an answer

In all questions it is important to structure your answers carefully. This will help you to explain your ideas as clearly as possible.

 Use the question

The bullet points in Paper 1, Question 2 give you a list of features to discuss. Making at least one point about each of these features will help you to give a detailed and varied response.

 Worked example

Look in detail at **lines 12 to 15** of Source E on page 95.

How does the writer use language here to describe the family home?

You could include the writer's choice of:

* words and phrases
* language features and techniques
* sentence forms. **[8 marks]**

The writer uses unpleasant verbs such as 'streaked', 'bulged' and 'seeped' to describe the house. This presents it as alive but also wild and uncared for. The language suggests that Rahel finds the house unwelcoming and is not happy to be back.

Similarly, the 'old house' is personified as wearing its roof 'pulled over its ears like a low hat'. This creates an image of it trying to shelter from the weather. The 'low hat' may also look unfriendly, as if the house wants to be left alone. Again, these language choices suggest it is unfriendly and unloved.

The metaphor of 'slanting silver ropes' of rain that 'slammed into the ground' makes the rain sound powerful in contrast to the damp 'old house'. The writer adds the simile 'like gunfire' to build up this feeling of power. It makes the weather sound frightening and the house feel unsafe.

Each sentence in these lines begins with a noun phrase that focuses the reader's attention on one detail of the scene: the rain, the earth, the roof, the walls and finally the garden. This builds up a clear picture, detail by detail, and creates the impression that Rahel is looking around, noticing all the different things about the home she has come back to.

In each paragraph, use the **what**, **how**, **why** structure to fully explore your points.

Make clear links between your ideas to show how the writer's language choices have a cumulative effect.

 Structuring paragraphs

Use a separate paragraph for each point you make. In each paragraph, you should:

* identify what choice the writer has made
* explain why they have made that choice
* suggest how this might have an effect on the reader.

 Planning

Make a quick plan by annotating the source and then numbering the three or four most significant ideas. You could organise your points in the order of the bullet points in the question, in the order in which they appear in the source, or from the simplest to the most complex.

Get straight into explaining your main points. You do not need an introduction or conclusion for this question.

Use adverbs to connect your paragraphs and show how your ideas link together.

Try to comment on all three of the features in the bullet points. This answer is structured in the same order as the bullets, but you don't need to follow this order.

 Exam focus

For lower-mark questions such as Paper 1, Question 2, you do not need to write an introduction or a conclusion to your response. Instead, you should focus on explaining your main points effectively. However, it is advisable to include a brief introduction and conclusion in your answers to Question 4 of both papers.

 Practice

Plan at least three paragraphs in response to this exam-style question.

Look in detail at lines **1 to 8** of Source A on page 91.

How does the writer use language here to describe the weather?

You could include the writer's choice of:

* words and phrases
* language features and techniques
* sentence forms.

 Made a start **Feeling confident** **Exam ready**

Paper 1, Question 2

Look at this Paper 1, Question 2 worked example, then answer the exam-style question at the bottom of the page.

 Worked example

Look in detail at this extract from **lines 1 to 11** of the Source.

How does the writer use language here to describe the damage to the hotel?

You could include the writer's choice of:

• words and phrases

• language features and techniques

• sentence forms. **[8 marks]**

Use key words from the question throughout your answer to stay focused.

The extract begins with a minor sentence: 'The Grand Hotel'. This sounds like an impressive announcement, suggesting it is an important building. This is further highlighted by the use of the 'wedding cake' metaphor, which suggests that it is beautiful and very impressive. Wedding cakes also have connotations of celebration, suggesting that the hotel is usually a happy place. The reader is encouraged to see the hotel as something special, which makes the damage that follows even more shocking.

The mood suddenly becomes more dramatic and shocking when the writer uses personification in the disturbing image of the night sky eating 'into the roofline' of the hotel. This presents the hotel as a victim, making it sound weak and unprotected. The writer continues using personification, describing the hotel as having a deep 'wound'. This implies that the hotel has been physically injured, highlighting the violence of the explosion. It might also make the reader think of the people staying in the hotel, who are also victims of the event, helping to make the reader feel shock and horror at the situation.

The dramatic mood and the feeling of violence are enhanced by the series of single-clause sentences the writer uses to suggest the narrator's shock at the damage. It ends dramatically with the short single-clause sentence, 'It amounted to nothing.' This creates a feeling that the narrator is so stunned she is lost for words.

Source – High Dive

In this extract, the protagonist has just witnessed an explosion at a hotel.

The Grand Hotel. The brickwork wedding cake her father had encouraged her to admire so many thousand times. She was thinking of the cliché that you can't believe your eyes. The night sky had eaten into the roofline. The wound in the building went three floors deep. Smoke gushed up out of the dark space where rooms were supposed to live. The railings of balconies arced down, trailing off into nothing. Rubble tumbled in from left and right. She didn't know what had gone wrong with the rules of the world. She stood there with all she'd learned. It amounted to nothing.

Aim to cover all three bullet points from the question.

Use relevant subject terminology to explain the writer's language choices clearly.

Use carefully selected evidence to support each of your points.

For each of your points, explain **what** the writer has done, **how** they have done it, and **why** they have done it.

Develop your response further by exploring the effects and connotations of words in detail.

Make links between language choices that build up to create a combined effect.

 Exam-style practice

Look in detail at **lines 1 to 16** of Source D on page 94.

How does the writer use language here to describe the kites? **[8 marks]**

Structure

In Paper 1, Question 3, you will need to comment on the writer's use of structure.

Paper 1, Question 3

This question focuses on structure. You will need to think about the source as a whole and explore how the writer guides the reader through it. For example, you could consider how the structure causes the reader's feelings to grow and change as they read. Use the bullet points in the question to help you focus on the key points.

Worked example

You now need to think about the **whole** of Source C on page 93. This text is from the opening of a novel.

How has the writer structured the text to interest you as a reader? You could write about:

- what the writer focuses your attention on at the beginning
- how and why the writer changes this focus as the Source develops
- any other structural features that interest you.

[8 marks]

One way in which the writer uses structure to ◄ interest the reader is by focusing on everything except the missing woman. This creates a feeling of mystery and makes the reader want to know what has happened to her. This also creates humour because it is frustrating for the reader.

The extract begins with Mr Creasy out on the ◄ street looking for his wife, but very quickly moves inside the narrator's family home, where they are gossiping about Mrs Creasy's disappearance and not really taking it seriously. This might make the reader laugh or feel sorry for Mr and Mrs Creasy.

Most of the source is written in short paragraphs describing the family's actions and dialogue. This ◄ adds to the impression of them having a chat over breakfast and not taking the problem seriously, while Mr Creasy is 'marching up and down' with 'heavy shoulders' suggesting he is a lot more worried about his wife than the family around the breakfast table are. This contrast helps to build up tension.

The source ends with 'next door's cat'. This suggests that everyone has already forgotten about Mrs Creasy. However, the final sentence about how 'no one had seen it since' sounds ominous and adds to the feeling of mystery and tension.

Consider the impact the beginning and ending have on the rest of the text, bearing in mind that the source may be an extract.

Sentence level structure

You can analyse sentences in the structure question, but only in terms of how they affect the reader's journey through the source as a whole. For example, you could explore the significance of the first or last sentence, or the position of a sentence that reveals a sudden twist. Remember, you will not be awarded marks for comments on sentence form.

Whole text structure

It is a good idea to give a general overview of the source's structure and then analyse a few examples in detail. You could think about:

- ☑ beginnings and endings
- ☑ things that change, such as places or characters
- ☑ repeated ideas, words or phrases
- ☑ shifts in perspective, such as from one character to another
- ☑ shifts in time, such as flashbacks.

Paragraph level structure

At a paragraph level you could think about:

- ☑ the lengths of paragraphs – for example, a short paragraph emphasises a key idea or action
- ☑ the positioning of a particular paragraph in relation to the text as a whole, such as a first paragraph of description used to introduce the setting
- ☑ the reader's experience of travelling through the sequence of paragraphs – for example, how each paragraph adds to the reader's impression of a character.

Comment on the overall structure and then analyse a few examples.

Think about paragraph structure and its impact.

Think carefully about what the writer chooses to reveal when, and what effect this might have on the reader.

Exam-style practice

You now need to think about the **whole** of Source B on page 92.

This text is from the opening of a novel. How has the writer structured the text to interest you as a reader?

Openings and endings

For Paper 1, Question 3, you need to focus on the overall structure of the source. Looking at its opening and ending can be a good place to start.

Openings

The opening of an extract may:

- set the scene to help the reader feel as though they are really there
- introduce a character to help the reader quickly build a relationship with them
- plunge the reader directly into the action to create excitement
- withhold key information to build suspense and create questions the reader wants answers to.

Endings

The ending of an extract may:

- resolve all conflict to satisfy the reader
- leave a cliffhanger to create a sense of mystery and prompt the reader to imagine what might happen next
- link back to the beginning, using a cyclical structure to emphasise a key idea to the reader
- summarise events or ideas, or draw a conclusion to help the reader consider the text's message or theme.

Worked example

You now need to think about the **whole** of Source A on page 91.

This text is from the opening of a novel.

How has the writer structured the text to interest you as a reader?

You could write about:

- what the writer focuses your attention on at the beginning
- how and why the writer changes the focus as the extract develops
- any other structural features that interest you.

[8 marks]

The writer structures this extract by beginning and ending it in a similar way. This cyclical structure draws the reader's attention back to the behaviour of the characters. In the third sentence the writer talks about people standing 'in a huddle by the bolted door' and in the last sentence the writer repeats 'we stand in silence by the door'. This creates a sense of time going by, but also of nothing changing, because they are still doing exactly the same thing. The reader begins to feel tense because the people seem to be waiting for something and the reader knows from the very first sentence that a 'body' is about to be found, but nothing seems to be happening yet. This makes what follows seem even more exciting...

Comment on **why** the writer has done this by exploring the overall effect it may have on the reader as they progress through the text. Make sure you focus on the structure of the text only.

Aiming higher

You should think about the opening and ending in relation to the rest of the source.

The information and effects in the opening will influence how the reader reacts to what happens next. For example, a mysterious atmosphere might make them consider characters suspiciously, or prompt them to look out for clues.

Similarly, the ending can either confirm or challenge the reader's first impressions. Revealing a key piece of information in a final twist could cause them to rethink their interpretation of a character or situation. Consider how the ending may link back to the beginning.

Identify **what** the writer has done, using subject terminology (such as 'cyclical structure' or 'metaphor') and clear reference to the question.

Explain **how** the writer has done this by providing evidence to support your point.

Consider how the opening or ending affects the reader's response to the rest of the text.

Practice

Write one or two paragraphs in response to this exam-style question, focusing on the first three paragraphs of the Source.

You now need to think about the **whole** of Source E on page 95.

This text is from the opening of a novel.

How has the writer structured the text to interest you as a reader?

Sequencing

Sequencing is the order in which writers position and develop their ideas. You may wish to discuss it in your answer to Paper 1, Question 3.

 Structure

A **chronological** structure is where the writer describes events in the order in which they happen. This can be used to gradually develop characters and build tension.

A **non-linear** structure jumps back and forth in time. A writer could use this to create a sense of drama or to show how past and present events are linked.

 Order

You could think about:

- ☑ the order in which information is revealed, and how this creates suspense or surprise for the reader
- ☑ the order in which characters are introduced, and how this affects the reader's impression of them
- ☑ how ideas are ordered to develop one another, and how this causes the reader's opinions to grow and change as they progress through the narrative.

 **Positioning**

An idea or a piece of information can be positioned to have an impact on the reader when they reach that particular point in the text. It might surprise them, shock them or make them reconsider their opinion. For example, a character who doesn't say much might seem cold and unfriendly until the reader learns about their tragic past.

By placing certain ideas or events side by side, the writer can also highlight parallels and contrasts. This is called **juxtaposition**.

 Worked example

You now need to think about the **whole** of Source B on page 92.

This text is from the opening of a novel.

How has the writer structured the text to interest you as a reader?

[8 marks]

The writer sequences this description using a chronological structure that leads the character through each stage of the journey. This helps the reader to understand the narrator's boredom. Each paragraph describes a different part of the journey, first the 'ancient' track, then the scenery of 'warehouses and water towers', then the backs of houses and finally a phone ringing. These small details, positioned close together, build up to reflect the length of the journey, showing how boring it is. This makes the reader wonder what will happen next.

However, despite the changing focus, the reader's attention is brought back to the 'little pile of clothes' from the beginning, highlighting the narrator's fascination with it...

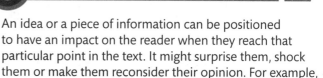 **Repetition and reiteration**

Repetition can be a feature of a writer's language (see page 6), but it can also be used as a structural device. Structural repetition often demonstrates the importance of something to the reader, such as a flashback that appears again and again. Repetition can also be used as a contrast to highlight change – for example, to show how a character's feelings about their family home change over time.

Reiteration is where something is repeated, but in slightly different ways. Writers often use this to weave themes through a story. If several characters in a story lose something, each in a different way, you could say that the theme of loss is reiterated throughout the text.

Use subject terminology such as 'chronological' to clearly explain the structure.

Use quotations or paraphrasing to support your ideas, but do not analyse the writer's language choices.

 Practice

Read **lines 22 to the end** of Source D on page 94. How does the writer sequence their ideas to reflect the excitement of the competition?

Explain the overall effect the reader's journey through the text might have on their thoughts and feelings.

Paragraphs and sentences

In Paper 1, Question 3, you can comment on paragraphs and sentences, but only when they contribute to the overall structure of the text.

② Paragraphs in structure

Looking at paragraphs is an effective way to explore how a writer has sequenced and linked their ideas. Ask yourself these questions:

- What does the reader learn in each paragraph?
- How does the focus of each paragraph change?
- How are the paragraphs linked?
- How might the reader's mood or opinions change as they travel through the paragraphs?

② Aiming higher

Cohesion is the way ideas are linked within and between sentences and paragraphs. Writers build cohesion by:

- using adverbials and conjunctions such as 'meanwhile', 'finally' and 'whereas' to guide the reader through the text
- maintaining a theme or semantic field, for example repeated use of words about nature.

Writing cohesively makes a text easy for the reader to follow. However, writers sometimes break cohesion for effect, for example to reflect a narrator's random, anxious thoughts or a series of mysterious, apparently unconnected events.

② Context

For Paper 1, Question 3, you must consider the specific impact of a structural feature at the point the writer has positioned it in the text. For example, a short paragraph could be used to:

- emphasise a surprising contrast to the longer paragraph that came before it
- emphasise the key idea in the longer paragraph that came before it
- summarise the key idea in the longer paragraph that follows it.

Always think about how a structural feature works in the context of the rest of the source.

② Sentences in structure

You can also think about how particular sentences contribute to the overall structure of the source. Ask yourself these questions:

- Why is this sentence placed where it is?
- Do any sentences reveal sudden changes or twists?
- How do **topic sentences** link the paragraphs?

A **topic sentence** is a sentence at the beginning of a paragraph that introduces the main idea.

⑩ Worked example

This text is from the opening of a novel.

How has the writer structured the text to interest you as a reader?　　　　**[8 marks]**

> **Source – All The Light We Cannot See**
>
> *This extract is from a novel set in the Second World War and describes an American bombing mission.*
>
> They cross the Channel at midnight. There are twelve and they are named for songs: *Stardust* and *Stormy Weather* and *In the Mood* and *Pistol-Packin' Mama*. The sea glides along far below, spattered with the countless chevrons of whitecaps. Soon enough, the navigators can discern the low moonlit lumps of islands ranged along the horizon.
>
> France.

The writer has structured the text to interest the reader by starting with the word 'they'. This creates a feeling of mystery as the reader does not know who these people are. The writer gives some clues that they are flying over the sea, describing the 'whitecaps' and the 'islands' they are approaching. Slowly building up this picture creates a feeling of tension.

The writer then contrasts this longer first paragraph with a very short second paragraph, which is just a one-word minor sentence: 'France.' This short paragraph makes it feel like there is something dramatic and maybe disturbing about what will happen when they get there...

⑩ Practice

Read **lines 37 to the end** of Source D on page 94.

How does the writer use sentences structurally to interest the reader?

Narrative perspective

Narrative perspective is the point of view from which the writer shows the action to the reader. Shifts in narrative perspective can be used to draw the reader's attention to particular information, to create contrast or to highlight themes and ideas.

② Focusing the reader

A writer chooses what the reader sees, how they see it and when they see it. When you analyse a text, pay close attention to what the writer focuses your attention on. It might be helpful to imagine the writer as a director with a film camera, using close ups, zoom and movement to guide the reader through the story.

② Revealing information

Writers often use a change in narrative perspective to draw the reader's attention to an important idea or piece of information. For example, a general description of a kitchen might slowly zoom in on a sharp knife glinting in the sun, implying to the reader that it is the murder weapon.

⑩ Worked example

You now need to think about the **whole** of Source E on page 95.

This text is from the beginning of a novel.

How has the writer structured the text to interest you as a reader? **[8 marks]**

One way in which the writer uses structure to create interest is by shifting the narrative perspective. The first three paragraphs use a zoomed-out perspective to provide an overall description of the weather and surroundings in Ayemenem. This gives the reader a clear picture of the setting.

In the fourth paragraph, the narrative perspective shifts to Rahel, suggesting that she is an important character and encouraging the reader to see the details through her eyes. The description zooms in by describing the garden and the animals living there, then moves on to the house. This creates a contrast because the garden is full of life, whereas the house looks 'empty' and 'bare'. This suggests that the house is unwelcoming, making the reader feel sorry for Rahel.

It is not until the final paragraph that we hear anything about Rahel's family, which is surprising considering that she is returning home after a long time. Even then, we learn about a 'baby grand aunt' that Rahel 'hadn't come to see'. Finally, in the last sentence, the focus shifts to Estha, who Rahel clearly cares about. Throughout the extract, it is as though the narrative is a searching camera, zooming in closer and closer to find something positive about the home. This suggests that Rahel and her brother have a difficult relationship with their family, making the reader wonder what happened to make Rahel return.

Consider the wider impact of the writer's choices. How might they make the reader reconsider what has already happened or how the story will develop?

② Structure

Shifts in narrative perspective can also be used across the whole of a text to shape its structure. Think about how the writer takes the reader on a journey.

You could consider why a shift in narrative perspective happens at a particular point, and how this affects the reader's reactions to the text. For example, a shift to a new character's perspective in the middle might reveal new information and cause the reader to rethink their opinion of what has already happened.

② Themes and atmosphere ⬆

Shifts in narrative perspective can emphasise a character's mood. Shifting the reader's focus from a boy's unhappy thoughts to the cheerful scene around him could draw the reader's attention to the boy's isolation, causing the reader to sympathise with him more.

Jumping between times, characters or storylines allows the writer to group related elements together, highlighting subtle links in theme that the reader might not otherwise notice.

Explain **what** the writer has done with narrative perspective and **how** they have done it

Try to explain the journey on which the narrative focus takes the reader. Here, words like 'first', 'next' and 'finally' show a clear progression through the text.

Explain **why** they have done this, thinking about the effect on the reader.

⑩ Practice

Read lines **1 to 11** of Source C on page 93. How does the writer use shifts in narrative perspective?

Paper 1, Question 3

Look at this Paper 1, Question 3 worked example, then answer the exam-style question at the bottom of the page.

 Worked example

You now need to think about the **whole** of Source D on page 94.

This text is from the middle of a novel. How has the writer structured the text to interest you as a reader?

You could write about:

- what the writer focuses your attention on at the beginning
- how and why the writer changes this focus as the Source develops
- any other structural features that interest you.

[8 marks]

The writer starts the extract by focusing the reader's attention on the kites, creating a vivid picture of the sky crowded with kites of all different colours. It also builds the reader's interest by making the reader feel tense about the competition when we learn that Hassan's hands are 'already bloodied by the string', which shows how much the competition means to the narrator and his friend.

There are repeated references to violence throughout the extract, for example, Hassan's 'bloodied' hands, a 'gash' and 'cutting'. In the second paragraph we hear about a 'fight breaking out'. These references repeatedly emphasise how important this competition is to all the people taking part.

In the middle of the extract, the writer shifts the perspective to the narrator's internal thoughts about his father, making the reader wonder what will happen to the narrator if he loses the kite competition. This helps to build tension but also introduces an interesting relationship between father and son.

The writer also makes repeated references to time, which guide the reader chronologically through the action. As the competition goes on, the times mentioned go from an 'hour' to 'thirty minutes' to just 'fifteen'. This is like a countdown for the reader, building up the tension as we get nearer and nearer to the end of the competition.

The tension increases even more in the final paragraph as the pace increases, with lots of short sentences to show the narrator's concentration: 'I didn't dare look up to the roof. Didn't dare take my eyes off the sky.'

Finally, the extract ends focused on the 'blue kite'. This strongly contrasts with the 'two dozen kites' that started the extract, highlighting just how far the narrator has come in the competition. It also leaves the reader with a cliffhanger, as the blue kite is the only thing that stands between the narrator and victory. This makes the reader want to find out who wins.

Exam focus

Use the bullet points to help you to structure your answer.

- The first bullet point encourages you to write about the focus of the source's opening.
- The second bullet point encourages you to identify how the focus changes and explore why this happens, for example through shifts in narrative perspective.
- The final bullet point reminds you to write about other structural features such as those outlined on pages 16–19.

You could structure your points in chronological order, exploring the source's structure from beginning to end.

For each point, identify **what** the writer has done, explain **how** they have done it (with evidence) and explore **why** they have done it, focusing on the effect on the reader.

Discuss the effect repeated ideas have on the extract as a whole.

Consider the sequencing of events, looking for juxtapositions, parallels and connections. Make it clear what effect these have on the reader.

Use subject terminology to write effectively about specific structural features.

Only analyse the structural impact of sentence choices and make sure you consider them within the context of the text as a whole.

 Exam-style practice

You now need to think about the **whole** of Source A on page 91.

This text is from the opening of a novel.

How has the writer structured the text to interest you as a reader?

[8 marks]

 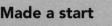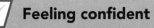

Evaluation

For Paper 1, Question 4, you will be asked to evaluate a source. You will need to make a personal judgement about it and then analyse how effectively the writer has achieved their intentions.

② Personal judgement

The question will provide you with a statement giving a student's response to the source. The first step is to decide whether you agree, partially agree or disagree with their response. Think about your own experience of reading the source and ask yourself these questions:

- Do I agree with the statement?
- Why?/Why not?

- What was the author trying to achieve?
- Were they successful?

⑩ Worked example

Focus this part of your answer on **lines 12 to 17** of Source B on page 92.

A student, having read this section of the text, said: 'The writer gives you a sense of how boring the train journey is. It makes you share in the narrator's frustration.'

To what extent do you agree?

In your response, you could:

- write about your own impressions of the characters
- evaluate how the writer has created these impressions
- support your opinions with references to the text.

[20 marks]

I agree that the writer successfully shows how boring and frustrating the train journey is.

One way the writer achieves this is through their choice of verbs to describe the train's movement. For example, 'crawls' implies that it is barely moving, while 'judders' captures how it stops and starts, never fully getting up to speed. These choices effectively combine to suggest a slow, boring journey.

The writer does not use adverbials to make any links between the sentences and paragraphs. This creates a disjointed, jerky effect, just like the movement of the train. Reading it, I felt like I was stuck on a slow, frustrating journey with the narrator.

The ordinary, everyday things the narrator sees out of the window add to the boredom: 'warehouses and water towers, bridges and sheds... modest Victorian houses'. The writer's use of a long list here reminds me of how things flash past when you look out of the window of a train, creating a strong visual effect...

② The writer's intentions

Once you have given your judgement, use the main body of your answer to support your opinion. You should:

- identify specific examples of how the writer has tried to achieve the intention described in the statement
- analyse these examples in detail to evaluate how effectively the writer has achieved that intention.

Exam focus

Focusing your answer on the statement in the question will help you to focus your thoughts and write an effective response.

The statement will suggest what the writer has done and the impact this has on the reader. Make sure you address both in your response.

Start with a brief overview of your personal judgement and how far you agree with the statement. You can build your judgement into your answers with adverbs like 'successfully', 'effectively', 'confidently' and 'intentionally'.

Then use the main body of your answer to support your opinion by analysing examples.

Draw on all your ideas from the earlier questions. You can discuss the writer's choices of both language and structure.

Think about your own experience as a reader when explaining the effect of the writer's choices.

⑩ Practice

Read the rest of Source B on page 92, from **lines 18 to 23**. Write one further paragraph continuing the answer to the exam-style question in the worked example.

Making a judgement

You should begin your answer to Paper 1, Question 4 by responding to a statement about the source.

 Do you agree?

Your response to the statement in the question will form the basis of your answer to Paper 1, Question 4. You can choose to agree, partly agree or disagree, but you must be able to support your opinion with detailed analysis of examples from the source.

The statement will draw your attention to one of the writer's key intentions, so there is likely to be more evidence to support agreement than disagreement.

 Exam focus

Remember that the main aim of this question is to evaluate how successfully the writer has achieved the intention described in the statement. Highlight the key words in the statement and the question, then use them frequently to keep your ideas focused.

Concentrate on exploring the ways in which the writer has tried to achieve their intentions and how successful they have been. Use your personal experience of reading the text to inform your analysis of this.

 Worked example

Focus this part of your answer on **lines 1 to 7** of Source D on page 94.

A student, having read this section of the text, said: 'The writer brings the boy's enthusiasm to life. It makes you share in his excitement.'

To what extent do you agree?

In your response you could:

- write about your own impressions of the boy
- evaluate how the writer has created these impressions
- support your opinions with references to the text.

[20 marks]

Overall, I agree that the writer effectively brings the boy's enthusiasm and excitement to life for the reader.

One way that the writer represents the boy's enthusiasm is through the way the kites are described. Positive visual imagery is created when the kites are described as 'red, blue and yellow'. These bright, primary colours remind me of a child's drawing. This colourful image creates a powerful feeling of excitement and clearly helps to explain the boy's enthusiasm...

However, the kites are also described using negative, aggressive imagery, such as the simile 'like paper sharks roaming for prey'. This could suggest that the narrator is being hunted and is at risk, making the kites seem frightening. Rather than sharing in the narrator's excitement, some readers might feel anxious or worried about the boy...

 Aiming higher

You can develop your answer by thinking about how other readers might respond to the source differently. Use adverbials such as 'however', 'in contrast' and 'on the other hand' to clearly signal that you are considering alternative interpretations.

If you take this approach, make sure that your overall opinion is clear and strongly presented in your answer.

Begin by introducing your personal response to the statement in the question. Then analyse examples to support your opinion

Explain **what** the writer has done to influence your opinion.

Identify **how** the writer has done this, using accurate subject terminology and evidence.

Suggest **why** the writer has made this choice, and how it affects you as a reader. Think about how successfully they have achieved their intention.

Use key words from the statement to keep the response focused throughout.

If relevant, develop your response by briefly exploring an alternative interpretation. Do not give an alternative interpretation for every point that you make.

 Practice

Read the **whole** of Source D on page 94. Identify two further pieces of evidence you could use to agree with the statement in the worked example.

 Made a start **Feeling confident** ✓ **Exam ready**

Narrative voice

'Narrative voice' is the voice that tells the story. It could be a character or a more general observer.

In fiction

In fiction texts, the narrative voice is not the same as the writer's voice. The writer's choice of narrator, and the ways in which the narrator tells the story, can have a significant effect on the ways in which the reader responds to the story and its characters.

First person narrator

First person narration is told by an 'I' who is usually the protagonist. They can observe events unfolding around them, express opinions and recall memories. This voice allows the writer to show the reader what the narrator is feeling and thinking. It can make the reader feel that they have a close, sympathetic relationship with the narrator.

Worked example

Focus this part of your answer on **lines 9 to 14** of Source D on page 94.

A student, having read this section of the text, said: 'The writer shows you the difficult relationship between the narrator and his father. It makes you want him to win the kite competition even more.'

To what extent do you agree?

In your response you could:

- write about your own impressions of the narrator's relationship with his father
- evaluate how the writer has created these impressions
- support your opinions with references to the text.

[20 marks]

I agree that the writer effectively shows you the difficult relationship between the narrator and his father. He describes 'stealing glances at Baba', which suggests he is afraid to look at him.

Because the writer has chosen to tell the story using a first person narrative, the narrator can tell us his thoughts and feelings, but has to guess his father's thoughts and feelings. For example, the narrator says he is not sure whether his father is supporting him, or hoping he will lose. This clearly shows that the narrator is not close to his father. The reader feels sorry for him, but also wants him to win to show his father that he can...

Remember to talk about the whole statement in your answer. This answer talks about the narrator's relationship with his father as well as whether the reader responds by wanting him to win.

Third person narrator

In a third person narrative, the narrator is able to show events from lots of different characters' points of view. The narrator may or may not take part in the action themselves. Characters in a third person narrative are referred to by their names or as 'he' and 'she'. This voice can encourage the reader to build a relationship with a number of characters, instead of just one.

Omniscient narrator

A third person narrator who knows everything, including the thoughts and feelings of the characters, is called an **omniscient narrator**. This voice can be used to give the reader a very detailed understanding of a situation. It can also be used to explore the relationships between characters and contrast their differing reactions to events.

Aiming higher

First person narrators have a limited view of events and may even withhold information or lie. This means that they may be **unreliable**. Writers can use this to create humour. Alternatively, they can give the reader a biased understanding of events, allowing the truth to be revealed in an exciting twist.

Sometimes, unreliability is made obvious: **My mother always told me if I said the sky was blue then she'd go outside and check. That's about how honest I am most of the time.**

In other cases, the reader must work it out for themselves: **Everyone else says Jim thought of it first, but they're remembering wrong. It was my idea.** This encourages the reader to think critically about the narrator and reconsider what they have read so far.

Use evidence from the text to infer details about the narrator and his father, then decide whether this information supports the statement in the question.

Practice

Read **lines 1 to 6** of Source B on page 92. Use the what, why, how structure to write a paragraph about the writer's use of narrative voice in the extract.

Made a start   **Feeling confident**   **Exam ready**

Setting

In Paper 1, Question 4, you could evaluate how effectively the writer uses setting to achieve their intention.

(2) Setting

Just like words, settings can have connotations. The location a writer chooses and the way in which they describe it can have a significant impact on the reader.

Settings can be used to create a particular mood or atmosphere. Settings can also reveal something about a character. For example, the setting of an old, dusty, crumbling house could have connotations of fear. It could also suggest that the reader should feel suspicious of, or sorry for, the person who lives there.

(2) Setting questions

When writing about setting, ask yourself:

☑ Where is the scene set? Does it have any connotations? For example, a graveyard might suggest death or fear.

☑ What is the weather like? Has the writer used pathetic fallacy to reflect a character's mood?

☑ What does the writer choose to describe? Does the narrative perspective draw your attention to particular things?

(10) Worked example

Focus this part of your answer on the extract from the Source below.

A student, having read this section of the text, said: 'The description makes the street feel very threatening. It makes you feel tense.'

To what extent do you agree?

[20 marks]

Source – Even the Dogs

In this extract, the policemen have just discovered a dead body.

The sky is darkening outside, a faint red smudge along the treeline by the river, the clouds stretching low and thin towards the ground.

The older policeman tugs at his shirt collar, pulling his tie away from his neck, muttering something to his colleague as he pushes past, leading the way down the cluttered hallway and out into the cold clear air.

I agree that the writer vividly describes the street as a threatening place. One way they do this is by using pathetic fallacy. The clouds 'stretching low and thin' create a disturbing mood reflecting the discovery of a dead body. This mood is reflected in the policeman 'pulling his tie away from his neck', suggesting he is feeling uncomfortable and threatened.

The description of the sky also creates an uneasy feeling about the street. The verb 'darkening' suggests danger and secrecy, and the metaphor 'a faint red smudge' hints at blood. Both these details successfully create an ominous and dangerous mood...

Think about what the setting suggests to the reader about the characters. If weather is described, look for pathetic fallacy.

Don't forget to explore more explicit or literal features of the text.

Analyse how descriptive and figurative language affect the reader's impression of the setting.

Consider how the setting affects your feelings about what might happen next.

(10) Practice

Write one paragraph on setting in response to this exam-style question.

Focus this part of your answer on **lines 1 to 11** of Source E on page 95. A student, having read this section of the text, said: 'The writer makes the nature in Ayemenem sound rich and lively. It makes you feel as if you are there.'

To what extent do you agree?

 Made a start   **Feeling confident**   **Exam ready**   25

Atmosphere

The atmosphere is the overall mood or tone of a text. It can be used to create a particular feeling in the reader.

 Atmosphere

Writers use atmosphere to influence the reader's response to a text. For example, if a scene has the happy, celebratory atmosphere of a birthday party, a mysterious package might seem exciting to the reader. In contrast, the same package could seem suspicious in a story with a bleak, dangerous atmosphere.

 Worked example

Focus this part of your answer on the extract from the Source below.

A student, having read this section of the text, said: 'The writer creates an ominous atmosphere in this extract. You share the character's unease, as though you are in the hospital with him.'

To what extent do you agree?   **[20 marks]**

Source 1 – The Day of the Triffids

This extract is from the start of a novel. The narrator has just woken up in hospital.

No wheels rumbled, no buses roared, no sound of a car of any kind, in fact, was to be heard. No brakes, no horns, not even the clopping of the few rare horses that still occasionally passed. Nor, as there should be at such an hour, the composite tramp of work-bound feet.

The more I listened, the queerer it seemed – and the less I cared for it. In what I reckoned to be ten minutes of careful listening I heard five sets of shuffling, hesitating footsteps, three voices bawling unintelligibly in the distance, and the hysterical sobs of a woman. There was not the cooing of a pigeon, not the chirp of a sparrow. Nothing but the humming of wires in the wind...

I agree that the writer successfully creates a sense of unease. They do this by establishing a tense, ominous atmosphere. For example, they repeatedly use negative words like 'no', 'not', 'nor' and 'nothing'. Together, these suggest how unusual and disturbing the quiet is, highlighting the narrator's fear and making me wonder what has happened.

In addition, by listing all the sounds that are missing, the writer clearly emphasises how many things feel wrong. Not knowing what is going on outside makes me uneasy, just like the narrator.

The tense atmosphere is developed by the few sounds that the narrator can hear. In a hospital, I'd expect to hear machines, and doctors and nurses talking. In contrast, the 'shuffling', 'bawling' and 'sobs' are not reassuring and the constant 'humming' seems eerie...

 Getting an overview

To identify a text's atmosphere, you need to think about how the writer's choices build up to create an overall feeling. Identifying the atmosphere can be a useful overview to start with in your answer. You can then develop your response by exploring examples of how the writer has created it.

① **Elements of atmosphere**

Atmosphere can be created through:
- ☑ setting
- ☑ characters
- ☑ dialogue
- ☑ objects
- ☑ actions.

Consider beginning your answer with an overview of the atmosphere and then analysing some examples in detail.

Use specific examples to back up your more general ideas about atmosphere.

Clearly explain how the atmosphere affects your experience of the text.

Think about what the writer has chosen to leave out too. In this example, the missing everyday sounds have a dramatic effect on the atmosphere.

 Practice

Plan your answer to this exam-style question.

Focus this part of your answer on Source A on page 91. A student, having read this text, said: 'The writer creates a mysterious atmosphere. It makes you wonder what is going on.'

To what extent do you agree?

Character

When you are evaluating how successfully a writer has created a character, think about all the different methods the writer has used to reveal that character's personality to the reader.

② Character

When analysing character, think about these elements:

- ☑ **Physical description** – what physical characteristics has the writer chosen to describe and what language have they used to describe them?
- ☑ **Action** – how do they act and what verbs does the writer use to describe their actions? How do other characters react to them?
- ☑ **Narrative voice** – is the story told from their perspective? If so, what is the effect of this?
- ☑ **Dialogue** – how do they speak and what do they say? How do other characters speak to them?

② Characterisation

Writers can **directly** tell the reader about a character: Wayne was very kind and thoughtful. This might be used to quickly develop the reader's picture of a character.

Writers can also **indirectly** suggest information: Wayne went to visit his grandmother in hospital. This might encourage the reader to think more deeply about the character and could help to build a stronger understanding of them.

Writers often develop characters and their relationships through dialogue. "You look exhausted, Mum," said Wayne, smiling anxiously. "You put your feet up and I'll go and visit Grandma."

⑩ Worked example

Focus this part of your answer on the extract from the Source below.

A student, having read this section of the text, said: 'The writer creates a larger-than-life image of the uncle. It really makes you warm to him.'

To what extent do you agree?   **[20 marks]**

> **Source – A Moment in Time**
>
> *In this section, a narrator describes his uncle.*
>
> He came sweeping in like a big hairy whirlwind. His heavy reddish-brown tweed suit matched his thick coarse hair, which not only came down low over his forehead but sprouted in lush gingery watch-springs from his ears and nostrils.

One way the writer clearly shows the uncle as 'larger than life' is through the description of his actions. The use of the verb 'sweeping' suggests that he moves quickly and confidently. The hyperbole of the simile 'like a... whirlwind' makes him sound impossibly large, like a force of nature. The combination of these images creates the impression that the character is very enthusiastic and hard to ignore.

The writer also uses a comical physical description, describing the hairs sprouting from the uncle's ears. This is usually an unpleasant sight, but the word 'lush' here suggests to me a more positive impression – he seems healthy and full of life...

⑩ Worked example

Focus this part of your answer on **lines 9 to 14** of Source D on page 94.

A student, having read this section of the text, said: 'The writer conveys a strong feeling of nervousness. This helps you to empathise with the boy'.

To what extent do you agree?   **[20 marks]**

The first person narration allows the writer to reveal the boy's thoughts and feelings. This more effectively helps the reader to understand his worries and insecurities. The questions the boy asks himself in line 10 about whether his father wants him to succeed or to fail help me to understand his motivations and increase my empathy for him. I know that he is scared of failing, so I hope he wins.

Furthermore, the narrator doesn't speak to anyone in this extract but frequently asks himself questions, making him seem isolated and insecure. Again, this makes me feel sorry for him...

⑩ Practice

Write two paragraphs in response to this exam-style question.

> Focus this part of your answer on **lines 14 to 21** of Source D on page 94.
>
> A student, having read this section of the text, said: 'The writer presents the narrator as brave. It makes you want to cheer him on.'
>
> To what extent do you agree?

Paper 1, Question 4

Look at this Paper 1, Question 4 worked example, then answer the exam-style question at the bottom of the page.

(10) Worked example

Focus this part of your answer on **lines 1 to 16** of Source A on page 91.

A student, having read this section of the text, said: 'The writer builds a sense of tension and suspense. It is as if you are there on the street, waiting to see what is inside the flat.'

To what extent do you agree?

In your response, you could:

- write about your own impressions of the mood created
- evaluate how the writer has created these impressions
- support your opinions with references to the text.

[20 marks]

I agree that the writer successfully creates tension and suspense from the start of the extract. By choosing to reveal in the very first sentence that a body has been found, they throw the reader into the action, establishing a tense, expectant mood.

Similarly, the writer's use of the inclusive pronoun 'we' makes me feel as if I am part of the 'huddle' of watchers. This helps to make me feel as if I'm actually there on the street and waiting to see what happens next, which again builds tension.

One way that the writer 'adds to the suspense is by presenting the setting itself as threatening. The air is described as 'vice-like' and the sky as 'scouring'. These adjectives powerfully suggest an aggressive, menacing atmosphere.

The writer adds to this atmosphere by suggesting that the street is not very busy. The writer describes the street as 'quiet' and we are told that cars only pass 'from time to time'. It's so quiet that you can hear the 'sighs' of someone's central heating, which suggests unhappiness, and the sound of someone hammering at a fencepost in the distance. The quiet and these sounds make me feel uneasy because the area seems deserted and dangerous...

(2) Planning

Question 4 is worth twenty marks, and you should spend about twenty minutes on it. It is worth spending about five minutes annotating the source and planning your answer so that you can write a well-structured response.

Begin your answer with a clear opinion on the statement. Make sure you can support your judgement with analysis of the source.

In the main body of your answer, analyse examples from the source to support your judgement. Remember to focus on how successful the writer has been in achieving the intention identified in the statement.

Think about your own experience of reading the text to help you evaluate how successful the writer has been.

Remember to address both parts of the statement.

Your answer to Question 4 should draw on all your ideas from the previous questions. You can discuss language and structure, as well as more general features such as setting, atmosphere and character.

Use carefully chosen evidence to support your points.

Use synonyms to vary your language and avoid sounding repetitive.

(10) Exam-style practice

Focus this part of your answer on Source E on page 95.

A student, having read this text, said: 'The writer creates a clear picture of a neglected, run-down house. It makes you feel sorry for Rahel.'

To what extent do you agree?

In your response, you could:

- write about your own impressions of the house
- evaluate how the writer has created these impressions
- support your opinions with references to the text.

[20 marks]

Made a start | Feeling confident | Exam ready

Types of non-fiction text

For Paper 2, Section A, you will read two literary non-fiction texts on a linked theme. One will be from the 19th century and the other will be from either the 20th or 21st century.

Form

Non-fiction texts are always written about facts or real life experiences. Literary non-fiction texts use techniques more often associated with fiction, such as similes, metaphors and narrative focus, to create interest for the reader.

Audience

The audience is who a text is written for. It can affect the writer's:

- tone (the overall mood)
- style (their language choices)
- register (how formally they write).

For example, a text written for teenagers might use a humorous tone, a relaxed style with lots of slang words, and an informal register.

Purpose

The purpose of a text is the effect the writer wants it to have on the reader. Many texts will have more than one purpose. Non-fiction can be written to:

- inform
- entertain
- instruct
- explain
- persuade
- argue.

Purpose affects the language and features a writer uses. A text presenting a point of view might use rhetorical questions, facts and dramatic language choices, whereas an instructional text will have short sentences, diagrams and clear language.

Form

Review

A review expresses an opinion about something, such as a restaurant or a film. It will usually inform, describe, entertain and advise. The formality and tone will depend on the audience and subject matter.

Diary or blog

A diary or blog provides a personal, informal account and is usually written in the first person.

Travel writing

Travel writing is written to entertain, advise and persuade. It usually includes detailed descriptions of place and character. The tone is likely to be personal, as the writer is recounting their own experiences.

Essay

Essays are written to present an argument or persuade the reader to agree with a point of view. They are usually formal and include evidence such as facts and expert opinions.

Autobiography or biography

In an autobiography, a writer describes their own life and experiences, whereas in a biography they give an account of someone else's life. These types of text are usually written to inform and entertain, and may use literary language to bring the story to life for the reader.

Article

Articles can be written to inform, entertain or persuade. The level of formality will depend on whether they are written for a tabloid newspaper, broadsheet newspaper or magazine. They may include features such as a headline or subheads.

Letter

Letters can be formal or informal, depending on their purpose and intended audience. They follow a set structure, starting with a salutation ('Dear...') and ending with an appropriate sign off ('Yours sincerely'). They are usually written to inform, argue or persuade, and often express an opinion very explicitly.

Aiming higher

The language used in 19th-century texts will seem very formal and may include some unfamiliar vocabulary. You could do some research into the views of 19th-century society to improve your understanding.

Practice

Spend at least 10 minutes each day reading from a variety of non-fiction sources. As you read, consider the form, audience and purpose of the text.

 Made a start 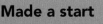 **Feeling confident** 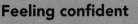 **Exam ready**

Interpreting unfamiliar vocabulary

In both papers, you may need to work out the meanings of unfamiliar words in the sources. Use these two techniques to help you tackle them.

 Root words

A root word is the core that a more complicated word is based on. You can find a word's root by removing its suffix and/or prefix.

If you recognise the root, or it reminds you of another word you know, you can use this to work out the meaning of the unfamiliar word.

- A **prefix** is added to the start of a root word to create a new word with a different meaning: for example, un + known = unknown.

  Here, the prefix 'un' changes the root word to the opposite meaning.

- A **suffix** is added to the end of a root word to change its word class. In this example, the suffix 'ish' changes a noun into an adjective: child + ish = childish.

  A suffix may also alter the tense or person of a verb.

The root of the word 'grandeur' is 'grand', which is an adjective meaning 'impressive' or 'magnificent'. This suggests that 'grandeur' is a noun meaning 'grandness'.

Source – The Great Exhibition
This extract is from a letter written in 1851. It describes a visit to the Great Exhibition.

> It is a wonderful place — vast, strange, new and impossible to describe. Its **grandeur** does not consist in one thing, but in the unique **assemblage** of all things.

'Assemblage' has the same root as 'assembly', which is a gathering of people. This suggests that an 'assemblage' is a gathering together of people or things.

 Context clues

You can also look at the context of an unfamiliar word to help you work out its meaning. Read the sentence containing the unfamiliar word and imagine that you have to fill in the blank.

Source – The rearing and management of children
This text is from a 19th-century household guide.

> If children were left to their own choice, they would be eating and drinking **perpetually** of whatever came in their way, till the stomach could no longer retain the **improper** substances. Wholesome food would be rejected for more **palatable** sweets and dainties. Before long, **depraved** tastes would be confirmed. Much the same **misfortune** sometimes befalls over-fed children of the wealthy, notwithstanding the care **bestowed** in other respects on their nurture; and an **impaired constitution** is the result.

  Aiming higher

Record the meanings of unfamiliar words in a personal dictionary of tricky vocabulary. You could also make a list of the meanings of common prefixes and suffixes.

The word 'perpetually' is used to describe how children would eat if they could choose for themselves. It is followed by 'till the stomach could no longer retain', which implies that they would eat too much. This suggests that 'perpetually' means 'constantly'.

'Palatable' is used to describe 'sweets and dainties' and is contrasted by 'wholesome food'. This suggests that it means 'appealing' or 'appetising'. If you know that 'palate' means a person's sense of taste, you could also use this root word to help you.

'Constitution' can mean either a law, the physical makeup of something, or a person's health. The context of eating and children makes it clear that here it refers to health.

 Practice

Use the techniques given on this page to work out the meanings of these words in the extract from 'The rearing and management of children' above: improper; depraved; misfortune; bestowed; impaired.

  Made a start **Feeling confident** **Exam ready**

Skimming and scanning

Skim reading is where you quickly read through a text to find the main ideas. Scanning is a way to find a specific piece of information in a text. These skills are useful in both papers, but especially in Paper 2, where you have two sources to deal with.

② Skimming

Skimming is an effective way to familiarise yourself quickly with the texts before you start answering the questions. In the exam, you should read the questions; skim read the texts to get an overview of the main ideas, purpose and target audience; and then read the texts thoroughly.

When you skim, you don't have to read every single word. Instead, you should look at the following things:

- the heading or title
- the first paragraph
- the first line of every paragraph
- the last paragraph

② Scanning

When answering the questions, you can scan the texts to find a particular device, quotation or piece of information.

1 Decide what key words you are looking for. For example, you could find examples of statistics by looking for numbers.

2 Focus on looking for your key words only. You do not need to read every word.

3 When you find what you are looking for, check the context to make sure you fully understand it.

② Exam focus

Read the questions and underline the key words before you start skimming or scanning. This will show you what to look for in the texts.

⑩ Worked example

Read again the first part of **Source G** from **lines 1 to 14**.

Choose **four** statements below which are TRUE.

- Shade the boxes of the ones that you think are true.
- Choose a maximum of four statements.

[4 marks]

Skim the first line of each paragraph to identify the writer's overall attitude. Here, words like 'secret' and 'shameful' clearly suggest embarrassment, so this statement is true.

A. The writer is embarrassed that they once employed domestic help.

B. The writer paid to have her house cleaned seven days a week.

Scan the text to look for specific information like numbers. The word 'seven' is not in the source, but 'five' is, so this statement is false. Always be aware of context. In this example, 'every day' means every weekday, not every day of the week.

C. The writer believes that many people hire cleaners.

D. The writer used to be a cleaner herself.

E. The writer thinks the au pairs were rude.

F. The au pairs were bad cooks.

G. The writer thinks her au pairs benefited from the job too.

H. The writer employed au pairs for five years.

Skim the last line of each paragraph to identify the writer's key points. In the last line of paragraph four, the writer says that '80% of the middle-classes prefer to pay somebody else to do these tiresome chores'. This means that the statement is true.

⑤ Practice

Spend one minute skim reading Source I on page 99. Then sum up the main ideas in three sentences or less.

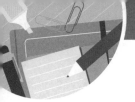
Paper 2, Question 1

For Paper 2, Question 1, you will need to identify explicit and implicit information in a source. Look at this worked example, then answer the exam-style question at the bottom of the page.

15 Worked example ✓

Read again the first part of **Source M** on page 103 from **lines 1 to 15**.

Choose **four** statements below which are TRUE.

- Shade the boxes of the ones that you think are true.
- Choose a maximum of four statements.

[4 marks]

A. The writer thinks short holidays are best. ◯

B. The writer believes that travellers should be open to other cultures. ⬤ ←

C. The writer likes to travel in his own country. ⬤ ←

D. The writer always hitchhikes to exotic locations. ◯

E. The writer believes that there are exotic locations to visit in Britain. ⬤ ←

F. The writer flies from Luton Airport every year. ◯

G. The writer's children love staying in hostels. ◯

H. The writer is happy to go outside his comfort zone. ⬤ ←

2 Exam focus 📌 ✓

This question is worth four marks, so you should spend about five minutes on it. However, don't be tempted to rush. Read all the options carefully before making your selections.

First, eliminate any statements that are obviously false. Then work through the other options, making a small tick or a cross in the margin next to each one. Only shade in the boxes when you have made your final decision.

> Skim the first line of each paragraph to get the main idea. In this example, the information is explicit in the first line of the source.

> Use skimming to build up an overall impression and identify inferred information. In the source, this information is implied in paragraphs two and three, where the writer talks positively about travelling in the UK.

> Scan for key words to find specific information. In the source, the phrase 'exotic locations' is used to describe areas of the UK, so this statement is true.

> Check the context to ensure you understand how the key words are being used. In the source, the phrase 'comfort zone' can be found by scanning. However, the reader has to infer from 'I sometimes do this' that the writer is happy to leave his comfort zone.

5 Exam-style practice ✓

Read again the first part of **Source J** from **lines 1 to 14** on page 100.

Choose **four** statements below which are TRUE.

- Shade the boxes of the ones that you think are true.
- Choose a maximum of four statements.

A. The writer thinks that civilised people should eat at the same time each day. ◯

B. The writer feels that meal times should be a social event. ◯

C. The writer says that mealtimes are more important than prayers. ◯

D. The writer believes that having bad table manners creates a bad impression. ◯

E. The writer thinks that if families did not eat and pray together they would rarely all be together. ◯

F. The writer says that it is acceptable to be late to the dinner table. ◯

G. The writer says that you should finish what you are doing before you sit down to eat. ◯

H. The writer thinks that the dinner table is a place where good manners can be taught. ◯

[4 marks]

✓ **Made a start**   ✓ **Feeling confident**   **Exam ready**

Synthesising two texts

Paper 2, Question 2 will ask you to synthesise information and write a summary. Start by planning your answer.

(2) The texts

To 'synthesise' means to bring together information from different sources into something new. For Paper 2, Question 2, you will need to write a summary of the similarities or differences between two texts.

You should:

- make statements about clear similarities or differences between the sources
- select details from both sources to use as evidence
- make clear inferences about both sources.

(2) Getting started

1 Read the question and underline the key words to identify the focus.

2 Skim read the longer source, underlining any relevant evidence.

3 Skim read the second source, underlining any relevant evidence.

Go to page 31 to revise skimming and scanning.

(2) Planning your answer

When you have identified evidence in both texts, you need to organise it. Briefly read through your evidence again, and then make a list or table of the key similarities or differences. Think about what your evidence implies as well as what it explicitly says. Go to page 7 to revise inference.

Question 2 is worth 8 marks, so you should concentrate on the three or four most significant points.

(1) Exam focus

The question will always ask you to summarise either similarities or differences, never both. Read it carefully and focus on what it asks for.

Use a style of plan that works for you. It could be a spider diagram or rough jottings around the sources, rather than a list or table.

(10) Worked example

You need to refer to **Source L** on page 102 and **Source M** on page 103 for this question.

Use details from **both** Sources. Write a summary of the differences in the narrators' experiences of travel. **[8 marks]**

Plan

Source L	Source M
• Travelling around the world – 'tour around the world'	• Travelling in the UK – 'on holiday to Scotland'
• Travelling by ship – 'on my way to the ship'	• Sometimes hitchhikes or cycles – 'hitchiking, cycle touring'
• Travelling alone – 'moving away from all I knew'	• Travelling with his children – 'every year I take my kids on holiday'
• Travelling to break a world record	• Travelling to explore unusual places, e.g. Birmingham – 'can't be satisfied with resorts, museums and tourist attractions'
• Feels homesick already – 'I had a sentimental longing'	• Enjoys seeing and experiencing new things – 'this sense of curiosity'.

Write your ideas in short notes. You do not need to write in sentences. Rather than writing out the quotations you want to use, you could underline or highlight them on the actual sources.

Match up related points side by side in the table, or draw lines to connect them.

Focus on similarities or differences that are relevant to the question.

Include any inferences you make from the sources. See page 7 to revise how to infer.

(10) Practice

Find three differences you could use in your answer to this exam-style question.

You need to refer to **Source F** on page 96 and **Source G** on page 97 for this question.

Use details from **both** Sources. Write a summary of the differences in 19th-century and 21st-century servants.

Structuring a synthesis answer

When answering a synthesis question, you will need to structure your answer clearly to show that you are combining relevant information from both sources.

 Comparing the texts

You can compare the texts in two ways.

- Write about all the information in one text, then write about all the information in the other text.
- Compare both texts in each paragraph of your response.

The second option is more challenging, but makes your comparison much clearer as it focuses on one similarity or difference at a time.

 Exam focus

Always make it clear which source you are referring to. You can do this by:

- referring to each by name, for example: 'Source A' and 'Source B'
- using the writers' surnames
- referring to them by text type, for instance, 'the letter' and 'the article'.

Be consistent in the method you use and avoid copying out long titles.

 Using adverbials

Use adverbials to guide the reader through your synthesis and make links between the two texts.

Go to page 5 to revise word classes.

Similarities	Differences
Similarly...	On the other hand...
Likewise...	Whereas...
In the same way...	However...
Also...	Unlike...

 Showing inference

Inferring information is a key skill for Paper 2, Question 2. Use phrases like these to show where you are reading 'between the lines':

- Both texts suggest...
- This implies that...
- We can assume from this...
- We can infer that...

 Worked example

You need to refer to **Source F** on page 96 and **Source G** on page 97 for this question.

Use details from **both** Sources. Write a summary of the similarities between the employers.

[8 marks]

The employers in both sources think that housework is not their responsibility. The middle-class employers in Source F feel that housework is 'beneath them', which suggests they believe that they are too good for it and that someone of a lower class should do it for them. Similarly, the employers in Source G hire 'foreign students' to 'cook, clean, childmind, wash, iron and dog-walk' suggesting that they don't feel it is their responsibility to do housework either...

 Exam focus

Paper 2, Question 2 is a summary task. You do not need to:

- give your opinion about the topic
- draw on your own knowledge of the topic
- analyse language features.

Use a separate paragraph for each similarity or difference that you find. Begin each paragraph with a statement introducing the similarity or difference.

Then make a point about the first source.

Finally, make a point about the second source, using an adverbial to link it to your previous point.

For each point you make, quote or paraphrase evidence from the text and explain what you can infer from it.

 Practice

Write one paragraph in response to this exam-style question.

You need to refer to **Source H** on page 98 and **Source I** on page 99 for this question.

Use details from **both** Sources. Write a summary of the differences in the punishments described.

Paper 2, Question 2

For Paper 2, Question 2, you need to write a summary of the information in the two sources. Look at these two differently structured responses, then answer the exam-style question at the bottom of the page.

(15) Worked example

You need to refer to **Source J** on page 100 and **Source K** on page 101 for this question.

Use details from **both** Sources. Write a summary of the similarities in their advice about table manners.

[8 marks]

Model answer 1

Both sources say that children should learn at the dining table. Source K describes how children should 'grow up with a positive, happy, healthy, adventurous attitude to food'. In the same way, Source J claims that children can improve in both 'mind and manners' at the dinner table.

> Start with a topic sentence that clearly summarises a similarity. This will help to focus your answer.

> Select relevant information from the text and quote or paraphrase it to support your point. Briefly explain what you have inferred, but do not analyse the language.

The sources agree that it is important for children not to be fussy about their food. Source K calls children who are 'selective eaters' 'fussy beggars', implying that they are awkward and unreasonable. Similarly, Source J explicitly states 'avoid expressing your likes and dislikes'. This very clearly states that it is rude to complain about food.

> Use an adverb or adverbial phrase to introduce a similarity with the second source. This clearly shows that you are making a comparison.

> Refer equally to both texts. In this example, every point includes a quote and an explanation of the source texts.

Model answer 2

Source K advises that the dinner table should be a place for learning, claiming that it is at the table that children can foster a 'positive, happy, healthy, adventurous attitude to food'. It also suggests that it is important for children not to be fussy about their food. For example, it calls children who are 'selective eaters' 'fussy beggars', implying that they are awkward and unreasonable.

> This is an alternative way to structure your answer. First, explain all your points about one source.

> Use phrases like 'this implies' and 'this suggests' to signal that you are inferring information.

Like Source K, Source J states that the table should be a 'school of good manners', suggesting that children can learn from eating. Similarly, it agrees that children should not be fussy eaters. It explicitly states 'avoid expressing your likes and dislikes', making it very clear that it is rude to complain about food.

> Then explain all your points about the other source.

> It is very important to use adverbials to make clear links between the texts if you choose this structure.

(10) Exam-style practice

You need to refer to **Source L** on page 102 and **Source M** on page 103 for this question.

Use details from **both** Sources. Write a summary of the differences between the travellers. **[8 marks]**

Analysing language

In Paper 2, Question 3, you will need to analyse the language of a non-fiction text. Some features will be familiar from fiction texts (see pages 5–10), but others will be unique to non-fiction.

 ## Non-fiction language features

Non-fiction writers carefully choose their language to engage the reader and persuade them to agree with their opinion. Here are some examples of language features you might find in a non-fiction text.

Emotive language

A writer might choose particular language to create an extreme response or play on a reader's emotions: <u>Vulnerable</u> teenagers are <u>forced</u> to sleep rough on the <u>unforgiving</u> streets. Here, emotive language is used to make the reader sympathise with homeless teenagers.

Repetition

Patterns and rhythms within sentences are important features of rhetorical devices. A writer might repeat a word or phrase to highlight an idea: **Survival means thinking: <u>think</u> what you need, <u>think</u> how to get it, <u>think</u> what you will need next.** The repetition here emphasises the need for thought.

Direct address

Sometimes, the writer directly addresses the reader as 'you' to flatter or engage them: **<u>You</u> could walk to work, but <u>your</u> warm, dry car is just too tempting.**

Similarly, a writer may use the inclusive pronouns 'we' and 'us' to suggest that the reader and writer share the same thoughts and feelings: **None of <u>us</u> wants to walk to work when it's cold and raining.**

Colloquial language

Informal, conversational words or phrases can be used to build a connection with the reader: **Their attitudes need to change <u>pretty damn</u> quickly if they want to make a real difference.**

 ## Worked example

You now need to refer **only** to **Source G** on page 97.

How does the writer use language to try to influence the reader? **[12 marks]**

The writer begins by asking the reader to 'lean in and listen carefully'. The direct address immediately grabs the reader's attention and creates a sense of intimacy. It encourages the reader to accept the writer's point of view.

> For each point you make, identify **what** the writer has done and give evidence, explain **how** they have done it and suggest **why** they have done it, focusing on the effect on the reader.

This close relationship is developed through the use of colloquial language like 'jobbing journo'. This makes the writer sound down to earth and suggests that she doesn't take herself too seriously. Again, this gives the impression that the writer is friendly and likeable, making the reader want to trust her opinion.

> Think about how direct address engages the reader.

> Consider how colloquial language might affect the target audience.

The writer also repeats the word 'every' to emphasise how lazy she was to have a cleaner. This repetition might make the reader picture how dull it would be for the cleaner to do the same boring job in the same house every single day. It encourages them to sympathise with the cleaner.

> Look out for repeated words and phrases. Think about the significance and connotations of the repeated word, and the effect it might have on the reader. For example, it might emphasise a key point or suggest boredom.

Emotive language is used in a similar way. For example, the word 'lured' implies that people are tricked into moving to the UK. This makes them sound vulnerable, making the reader feel sorry for them and perhaps guilty if they employ a cleaner themselves...

> Clearly identify what emotion is created by emotive language and explore how this might shape the reader's reaction.

 ## Practice

Skim read Sources A–M on pages 96–103 and identify one example of each of the features on this page.

Rhetorical devices

Writers use rhetorical devices to emphasise their viewpoints and persuade the reader to agree with them.

 Common rhetorical devices

Pattern of three

A writer might use a trio of words or phrases to highlight or exaggerate a point. **Ice caps are melting, tides are rising and species are dying.** These three similarly structured statements highlight how widespread the effects of global warming are.

If there are two phrases that mirror each other, it is called parallelism, for example: **Eat well, live long.**

Hyperbole

Hyperbole is where a writer uses extreme exaggeration to emphasise a point or create humour: **Flying is awful. I hate having to arrive at the airport <u>two weeks early</u>, queue with <u>billions of people</u> and pay <u>£50 for a cup of coffee</u>.** This statement contains numbers that are obviously far too high, which makes the writer's frustration humorous and therefore more memorable.

Rhetorical question

Rhetorical questions do not require an answer and are used to challenge and engage the reader. For example, the rhetorical question **How would you survive without a supermarket?** encourages the reader to reflect on a service that is fundamental to many people's way of life.

List

A list of items or ideas can be used to highlight variety, quantity or enthusiasm, for example: **When you cross the line you feel like you're <u>limitless, immortal, indestructible, a real champion</u>.** This unusually long list of adjectives expresses how powerful the writer's experience was.

> When analysing non-fiction, you can also write about the figurative language techniques on page 9. Page 67 shows you how to use rhetorical devices in your own writing.

 Worked example

You now need to refer **only** to **Source K** on page 101.

How does the writer use language to try to influence the reader?

[12 marks]

The writer opens with the rhetorical question 'What are your rules at mealtimes?' This effectively engages the reader, encouraging them to think about their own opinions on the subject.◄

She then uses a list of adjectives, 'positive, happy, healthy, adventurous', to emphasise the importance she places on giving her children a good attitude to food and to persuade the ◄ reader to agree with her.

She also uses humour to lighten the tone and balance her argument. For example, she creates a vivid picture of how messy some children can be. A pattern of three is used in the adjectives 'slurpy, finger-licking, face-smearing' to convey her horror ◄ in a humorous way. This entertains the reader and shows them that the writer's views on relaxed eating are not unreasonable.

Humour is used to similar effect in the final paragraph, in the description of the writer's son taking an 'animalistic sniff of a frankfurter' before he eats it. The hyperbole leaves the reader with a funny image, but also suggests how proud the writer is of her children's relaxed attitude to food...

 Aiming higher

Sarcasm is where a writer expresses an idea in a mocking way by stating the opposite idea, such as saying 'love' when they mean 'hate'. To identify sarcasm, you need to look closely at the context of the words and the text's overall tone. **Irony** is also where a writer says the opposite of what they mean, but has a more light-hearted, humorous effect.

> Consider the position of rhetorical questions. They are often placed at the beginning or end of a text to have the strongest impact on the reader.

> Lists can be used to create many different effects. Make sure you clearly explain how your example specifically affects the reader.

> Consider how a rhetorical device could have multiple effects. This pattern of three forms a humorous description, and is also an example of hyperbole.

> Hyperbole often creates humour, but look out for other additional effects or meanings too.

 Practice

Skim read Sources A–M on pages 96–103 and identify one example of each of the rhetorical devices on this page.

 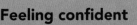

Tone, style and register

When you analyse the language of a non-fiction text, you should comment on its tone, style and register.

② Identifying tone

Tone refers to the way the writer expresses their attitude in a piece of writing. You can identify it by thinking about the tone of voice the writer might use to read their text out loud. Analysing style and register is an effective way to explore the tone of a text.

② Style

Style is created through language choices, sentence forms and structure. A writer will choose their style based on the form, audience and purpose of their text. For example, a blog might have a conversational style to entertain readers, whereas a newspaper article might have an informative style to appear reliable to readers.

② Register

Register is the formality of a text's language. Like style, it is affected by form, audience and purpose. For example, a formal register would be suitable for a letter to a headteacher, whereas an informal register would be more appropriate for a review in a young person's magazine. The time in which something was written also affects formality – 19th-century texts will usually sound more formal than modern ones.

② Formal register

Formal features include:

- ✓ Standard English
- ✓ sophisticated and/or technical vocabulary
- ✓ a greater number of long, multi-clause sentences
- ✓ precise adverbials to link ideas ('consequently', 'therefore', 'as such')
- ✓ the passive voice (**The thieves <u>were last seen</u> at the train station.**)

② Informal register

Informal features include:

- ✓ non-Standard English, such as regional dialect
- ✓ slang (**It cost me fifty quid.**)
- ✓ colloquial language (**That new car film is well lame.**)
- ✓ contractions (**won't, haven't**)
- ✓ a greater number of short, single-clause sentences.

⑤ Worked example

You now need to refer **only** to **Source G** on page 97.

How does the writer use language to try to influence the reader? **[12 marks]**

The writer starts in an informal register, using humour and colloquial words like 'spritzed'. This creates a friendly tone, which engages the reader by making them feel they are listening to someone they like and trust.

However, the tone becomes more serious towards the end of the article. The modal verb 'should' creates a stronger, more forceful tone. This change in tone, and the evidence the writer has used from a report, signals to the reader that this part of the article conveys a serious message...

② Aiming higher

Writers can use unexpected words to create a sarcastic or ironic effect. However, the overall tone of a text is important in helping the reader detect what is happening. For example, **It's a real honour** would sound sarcastic in a teenager's diary entry about having to tidy their room, but would sound sincere in a passionate speech. Go to page 37 to revise sarcasm and irony.

① Exam focus

Be careful not to rely too heavily on words like 'negative' and 'positive' when describing tone. Read widely and compile a list of descriptive words such as: 'lecturing', 'despairing', 'challenging' and 'light-hearted'.

⑩ Practice

You now need to refer **only** to **Source I** on page 99.

How does the writer use the tone of their writing to try to influence the reader?

Paper 2, Question 3

For Paper 2, Question 3, you will need to analyse the language of a source and the effect it has on the reader. Look at this worked example, then answer the exam-style question at the bottom of the page.

 Worked example ✓

You now need to refer **only** to **Source H**, on page 98.

How does the writer use language to try to influence the reader? **[12 marks]**

The writer begins in a serious tone, using formal language such as 'gentlemen' and long, multi-clause sentences to describe the scene. He also uses positive, attractive language to describe the 'bright sunshine' in the 'garden'. This creates a respectful but pleasant atmosphere, making the reader trust him.

The atmosphere begins to change in the next paragraph, where the description highlights the disturbing contrast between the vegetable garden, the gallows and the 'open grave'. These mixed images of life and death might give the reader an ominous feeling. The writer describes the gallows in great detail but refuses to name it, which clearly implies his disgust. It may take the reader a few moments to realise what it is, and when they do they are shocked.

The change in tone is completed when the writer describes the hangman himself. He uses the minor, exclamatory sentence 'But no such thing!' when discussing the hangman's lack of shame. This emphasises the writer's anger and disappointment.

The writer uses emotive language to show how disgusted he is by the gallows. The writer realises 'to my horror' that the man 'clothed in brown' is the 'designer of the horrible structure' and admits to a 'shudder' as he looks at the gallows, which suggests he is frightened and disgusted by them. Similarly, his emotive description of the victim as a 'struggling wretch' encourages empathy by focusing the reader on the hanged man and his suffering.

The writer contrasts his own disgust with the designer's pleasure at the sight of the gallows, often quoting his opinion, for example 'an excellent arrangement', and describing his gaze as 'admiring'. This contrast highlights his disgust and helps the reader to share in it.

 Key skills ✓

For Paper 2, Question 3, you will need to:
- ☑ demonstrate that you understand the effects of the language used
- ☑ use evidence from the source to support each of your points
- ☑ use accurate subject terminology.

Analyse style and register in detail to support your ideas about tone.

Structure your points carefully, identifying **what** has been used, **how** and **why**.

Make clear, relevant inferences to show good understanding of the effect of the writer's choices on the reader.

Use accurate subject terminology, such as 'exclamatory sentence'.

Exam focus

Remember that language analysis skills are transferable between Papers 1 and 2. In this question, you can talk about more general methods such as connotations, sentence structure and figurative language as well as exploring rhetorical devices.

Use precise, descriptive language in your comments.

Identify and explore rhetorical features.

Look beyond rhetorical devices. Here, the use of contrast and its effect are explored.

 Exam-style practice ✓

You now need to refer **only** to **Source L** on page 102.

How does the writer use language to describe her thoughts and feelings? **[12 marks]**

 Made a start   **Feeling confident**   ✓ **Exam ready**

Comparing non-fiction texts

Paper 2, Question 4 requires you to compare two non-fiction texts. You will need to identify similarities or differences in the writers' viewpoints and analyse how they are presented.

Similarities and differences

In the exam, the texts might be similar or different in a variety of ways. You could compare:

- the writers' viewpoints and ideas about the topic
- the writers' use of language
- the writers' use of structure
- the effects the texts have on readers.

Worked example

For this question, you need to refer to the **whole of Source F** on page 96, together with **Source G** on page 97.

Compare how the two writers convey their different attitudes to employing servants.

In your answer you could:

- compare their different perspectives and feelings
- compare the methods they use to convey their attitudes
- support your ideas with references to both texts.

[16 marks]

Both writers are critical of people who employ servants, arguing that they should learn to do some of the work themselves. However, they present their ideas in very different ways.

Source F is from a 19th-century household guide, written to advise the employers of servants how to run their homes. Because of this, the writer softens the criticism by speaking in general terms of 'many ladies'. They also make their comments constructive by saying how 'every mistress has it in her power' to make a difference. This empowers the women reading it, encouraging them to accept the criticism and change their ways.

In contrast, Source G is a modern newspaper article, intended to entertain rather than instruct. At first, the writer builds a positive relationship, like the writer of Source F does, but by using humour and an informal tone ('Lean in and listen carefully'). However, she then uses blunt language like 'dirty work', 'drudgery' and 'too posh' to shock the reader into reconsidering how servants are treated. This is very effective for a modern reader, who may have an emotional response to the dramatic changes in feeling and the extreme representation of ideas...

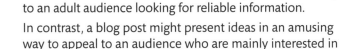 Audience, purpose and form

Audience, purpose and form will help you to explain some of the differences between the sources. A newspaper article might use lots of facts in order to appear trustworthy to an adult audience looking for reliable information.

In contrast, a blog post might present ideas in an amusing way to appeal to an audience who are mainly interested in the writer's personal point of view.

19th-century texts

Make sure you know which text is from the 19th century. You can discuss it from the perspective of a reader in either that period or the present day, but make sure this is clear in your answer.

Older texts often sound formal to modern readers, even if that was not the writer's original intention. If you make a point about formality, make sure it matches up with what you understand of the text's overall viewpoint.

Start your answer with a brief comparison of **what** the two writers' viewpoints are. In the rest of your answer you can then focus on **how** they present this and **why**.

Use the information provided with the sources to help you to understand their form, audience and purpose.

You should draw on your skills from the previous questions to help you compare how the writers present their ideas and why. You can think about their use of both language and structure.

Try to think about each writer's intended audience. How is the source specially tailored for that particular reader?

Practice

Identify three similarities you could refer to in your answer to this exam-style question.

For this question, you need to refer to the **whole of Source H** on page 98, together with **Source I** on page 99.

Compare how the two writers convey their similar attitudes to crime and punishment.

Viewpoints

Identifying and comparing the writers' viewpoints is a good starting point for Paper 2, Question 4.

② Identifying viewpoints

A writer's viewpoint is the way in which they look at a topic: their opinions about and attitudes towards the subject they are writing about. To identify the viewpoint of a text, skim read it and make a note of the key idea in each paragraph, then draw these ideas together to form a general overview.

⑩ Worked example

For this question, you need to refer to the **whole of Source H** on page 98, together with the **whole of Source I** on page 99.

Compare how the two writers convey their different attitudes to crime and punishment.

In your answer, you could:

- compare their different attitudes
- compare the methods they use to convey their attitudes
- support your ideas with references to both texts.

[16 marks]

Both writers are critical of how criminals are punished, however the writer of Source H focuses on the cruelty of the punishment whereas the writer of Source I focuses on ways to improve how criminals are treated.

Because Source I is a letter, the writer makes her opinion explicit right from the start: 'many local people are strongly in favour of this compassionate, practical new approach to rehabilitation'. This makes her argument seem well-organised and easy to follow, encouraging the reader to agree with it. In contrast, the writer of Source H makes his opinion less explicit. His account slowly reveals his disgust through emotive language like 'horror' and 'shudder'. This takes the reader on a powerful emotional journey, making them sympathise with his point of view.

In Source I, the writer uses statistics to support her ideas: 'Experts believe that 75% of prison inmates suffer from mental health issues'. This shows that she has a good understanding of the subject and that 'experts' agree with her, making the reader more likely to trust her opinion. In contrast, the writer of Source H gives an eyewitness account using 'I'. This shows the reader the situation from his point of view. It is as if the hanging is happening right in front of you, which makes you share the writer's shock and horror...

② Explicit and implicit viewpoints

In some texts, the writer's viewpoint is explicit in the title or the introduction. For example, the title 'Social media is bad for our health' may be a clear statement of the writer's viewpoint.

In others, the writer may not make their viewpoint clear immediately. They may slowly build their argument throughout the text and imply their viewpoint in the conclusion. This can draw the reader into their argument so they are more likely to agree with it.

> Begin with a summary of the two writers' viewpoints.

> Think about how explicitly each writer presents their viewpoint and explain the effect this has on the reader.

> After you have given a general overview, you can look at more specific examples of how the writers present their ideas to influence the reader.

> Continue your answer by exploring a few more examples of the writers' different attitudes and how they present them.

⑤ Practice

Annotate the texts in response to this exam-style question and identify the viewpoints of the two sources.

> For this question, you need to refer to **the whole of Source J** on page 100, together with **Source K** on page 101.
>
> Compare how the two writers convey their different attitudes to table manners.
>
> In your answer, you could:
>
> - compare their different attitudes
> - compare the methods they use to convey their attitudes
> - support your ideas with references to both texts.

Fact, opinion and expert evidence

Non-fiction writers present information in a range of ways in order to support their ideas and make their argument more persuasive or believable.

 Facts

A fact is something that can be proved to be true. Using facts suggests that a writer has a good understanding of their subject and has evidence to support their opinions. This gives their writing **authority**, making the reader more likely to trust their point of view. Facts can also help the writer to create a formal or serious tone in their writing.

 Bias

Bias is where a writer strongly represents just one side of an argument. In a humorous or entertaining piece of writing, this can be an effective way of engaging the reader and showing commitment to a point of view. However, in a more serious or informational text it may make the writer seem unreliable to the reader.

 Worked example

For this question you need to refer to **the whole of Source F** on page 96, together with **Source G** on page 97.

Compare how the two writers convey their similar attitudes to servants and their employers.

[16 marks]

The two writers have similar opinions about servants but present their ideas differently. The writer of Source G tells an anecdote using a humorous tone. This entertains the reader and helps build a strong relationship with them. The contrast when she adds in a statistic from a 'new survey' suggests that the text is not only entertaining but also supported by evidence, making her point of view more persuasive.

In contrast, the writer of Source F uses language alone to create an impression of authority. They use formal language such as 'the servant grievance' and long, multi-clause sentences to create a formal, serious tone. This makes the reader take their point of view seriously, even though it is not backed up by any evidence...

Opinions

An opinion is the writer's own personal view on a subject and is not necessarily based on fact or knowledge. Opinions can be serious, funny or shocking. A writer might try to influence the reader by supporting their opinion with evidence, or simply by presenting it as entertainingly as possible.

Expert evidence

Writers often use expert evidence in order to back up their opinions. This evidence could be facts, statistics from research, or quotations from a named expert. By demonstrating that an expert's opinion agrees with their own, a writer can makes their ideas more credible.

Anecdotes

An anecdote is a personal story based on the experience of the writer or someone they know. It can be used to add human interest and provide evidence in a less formal way than a fact or expert opinion.

When a writer adds weight to an argument by including a real-life story or an account from someone else, this is called **testimony**.

> Identify **what** the writer has done to present their point of view and **how** they have done it.

> Clearly explain **why** the writer has done this, focusing on how it might affect the reader. Try to go further than simply saying that a fact supports the writer's opinion. In this example, the student explains how the fact contrasts with the overall tone of the text, and considers how this effect builds on previous effects.

> Even if a writer doesn't use facts or expert evidence, you can consider **why** they haven't, or analyse what other techniques they use to convey their attitude instead.

 Practice

Read **lines 22 to 31** of Source K on page 101. Write a paragraph explaining how the writer uses expert opinion to influence the reader.

Comparing language

In Paper 2, Question 4, you need to refer closely to the writers' use of language to explain how they convey their viewpoints.

② Looking at language

When comparing the writers' methods, you can consider their use of language, including:

- ✓ rhetorical language features (go to pages 36 and 37)
- ✓ tone, style and register (go to page 38)
- ✓ words and phrases (go to page 6)
- ✓ sentence forms (go to page 10)
- ✓ connotations (go to page 8)
- ✓ inferred meaning (go to page 7)
- ✓ figurative language (go to page 9).

When you are comparing language, you can start by identifying **what** is similar or different.

Then, explain **how** this language choice is used in the first text. Quote or paraphrase an example.

Then, consider **why** the writer has done this, focusing on the effect it might have on the reader.

Finally, move on to the second text. Explain **how** the language choice is used and consider **why** the writer has done this. Use adverbials to clearly show comparison between the two texts.

Begin the process again for your next point of comparison. If it follows on from your previous point, use an adverbial to show this.

Don't be afraid to discuss features that are used in an unusual or surprising way. This shows high-level analysis of the texts.

If possible, link your points together to form a wider comparison of how the writers' language choices build up to create similar or different overall effects.

⑩ Worked example

For this question, you need to refer to the **whole of Source J** on page 100, together with **Source K** on page 101.

Compare how the two writers convey their different attitudes to table manners.

In your answer, you could:

- compare their different attitudes
- compare the methods they use to convey their attitudes
- support your ideas with references to both texts.

[16 marks]

Both writers use direct address to build a strong relationship with the reader. However, they do this in very different ways. The writer of Source J directs all their advice to the reader, repeating 'you' over and over again. Along with the text's serious tone and formal language ('vulgar habits', 'great improvement'), this creates a sense of an important lesson that the reader must learn. Interestingly, this effect reflects the writer's main point that the dinner table is 'a school of good manners'.

In contrast, the writer of Source K uses direct address to build a close, relaxed relationship with the reader. The colloquial language of 'fussy beggars to you and me' suggests a down-to-earth approach and makes the reader feel as though they are chatting with the writer as friends. Furthermore, the statement is a cheeky response to the NHS expert's phrase 'selective eaters'. This creates the opposite effect to Source J. It is as though the writer and reader are naughty students making a joke about their serious teacher.

Similarly, both writers use questions, but in very different ways. On the one hand, the writer of Source K begins with the rhetorical question 'What are your rules at mealtimes?' This encourages the reader to think about their own opinions. On the other hand, the writer of Source J also begins with two questions, but then answers them himself. This unusual question and answer pattern supports the feeling that the writer is a teacher and the reader is a learner...

⑩ Practice

Continue the model answer above with two further paragraphs comparing language in the sources.

Comparing structure

When comparing two writers' methods, you can write about their use of structure, as well as language.

 Worked example

For this question, you need to refer to the **whole of Source F** on page 96, together with **Source G** on page 97.

Compare how the two writers convey their different attitudes to servants.

In your answer, you could:

- compare their different attitudes
- compare the methods they use to convey their attitudes
- support your ideas with references to both texts.

[16 marks]

The two writers begin their texts differently. ◄ The writer of Source F begins by dismissing other discussions of the servant issue as 'to very little purpose' because they do not offer a solution. This suggests that the writer knows a lot about the topic, making them seem authoritative. It also implies that they are about to reveal a brand new solution, making the reader want to read on.

The writer builds up a feeling of anticipation as the reader waits to find out what this solution ◄ is. This sense of anticipation is developed in the next two paragraphs. The writer begins with a short, emphatic sentence: 'It used not to be so'. This implies that the treatment of servants can change, and it also delays revealing the solution a little longer. Having clearly outlined the problem, the writer finally begins to explain his advice in the fourth paragraph, which is clearly signalled by the words 'The first step in this direction is...'

While the writer of Source F slowly and clearly builds up to his argument, the writer of Source G can't wait to share her ideas. From the very first sentence, she grabs the reader with the instruction 'Lean in and listen carefully'. The next paragraph is only one sentence long, drawing attention to her secret but also suggesting how embarrassed she is by it. This opening is entertaining and informal, encouraging the reader to like and trust the writer.

However, the text is still very carefully structured. After the writer has developed this relationship with the reader, she introduces a fact to demonstrate that her personal experience is very similar to many others'. This neatly moves the text to a more general discussion of servants and how they are treated...

 Non-fiction structure

A non-fiction text will often be structured like this:

- **Introduction** – the writer sets out their main point and engages the reader's interest.
- **Development** – the writer presents increasingly complex ideas, supporting them with evidence and perhaps offering a counterargument.
- **Conclusion** – the writer sums up what they have said and leaves the reader with a memorable or thought-provoking ending to have a lasting effect.

You can revise this further on page 74.

Comparing how the two writers begin their piece can be a good place to start your answer.

 Features of structure

When comparing the writers' use of structure, you could think about:

- ☑ openings and endings (go to page 17)
- ☑ sequencing and cohesion (go to pages 18–19)
- ☑ paragraphs and the position of sentences (go to page 19)
- ☑ changes in tone (go to page 38)
- ☑ the positioning of facts, opinions and expert evidence (go to page 42).

Think about how the reader's first impressions from the opening shape how they react to what follows.

Think about the length and order of the paragraphs.

Consider how sequencing affects the reader's experience, for example by creating delay or surprise.

Look out for less obvious structural features, such as changes in tone or focus.

 Practice

Write one paragraph in response to this exam-style question, comparing the sources' conclusions.

For this question, you need to refer to the **whole of Source J** on page 100, together with **Source K** on page 101.

Compare how the two writers convey their different attitudes to table manners.

 Made a start **Feeling confident** **Exam ready**

Planning a comparative answer

Planning your comparison will help you to handle the two texts effectively and set out your ideas clearly.

Preparation

1. Start by skim reading both sources to identify the main ideas.
2. Then re-read each source in more detail, annotating anything that interests you about the language, structure and ideas.
3. Finally, read your notes and look for similarities and differences. You could underline or colour code the relevant evidence. Focus on features that you can compare directly.

Worked example

For this question, you need to refer to the **whole of Source J** on page 100, together with **Source K** on page 101.

Compare how the two writers convey their different attitudes to table manners.

In your answer, you could:
- compare their different attitudes
- compare the methods they use to convey their attitudes
- support your ideas with references to both texts.

Plan   **[16 marks]**

1. Overview – both want children to learn, but J thinks manners are important and K thinks playing is important.

2. Audience and purpose
   J – 19th-century guide for young women. Focused on manners and how people might judge you on your manners.
   K – modern article written by a parent. Focus on children enjoying food.

3. Direct address
   J – builds authority/distance from reader
   K – friendly, builds informal relationship

4. Language choices
   J – food and bad behaviour sound unappealing. Dull nouns.
   K – fun, physical verbs

5. Structure
   J – question and answer opening, then quite repetitive
   K – variety of methods – begins and ends with own children, shows how important they are

Structuring comparisons

You can structure your points of comparison in two ways:
- identify a similar feature used in both texts and compare the different effects it has
- identify a similar effect in both texts and compare how the writers achieve it in different ways.

Whichever structure you use, always make it clear which text you are talking about, and use adverbials to make links between the two texts.

Key features

Your answer should include:
- ☑ a short opening statement summarising the main ideas of the two texts
- ☑ a range of points comparing how the texts convey their attitudes
- ☑ evidence from both texts to support your ideas
- ☑ adverbials such as 'similarly', 'however' and 'in contrast' to link your ideas and show comparison.

The word 'methods' in the question refers to language, structure and form, and audience and purpose. Try to say something about each of these.

For each point, make a note about each text.

Keep your notes short and simple. You don't need to write in sentences.

Number your points to keep them in order. You could also number your annotations on the source to remind yourself what evidence to use for each point.

In the exam you should only spend about 5 minutes planning this answer.

Practice

Plan your answer to this exam-style question.

For this question, you need to refer to the **whole of Source H** on page 98, together with **Source I** on page 99.

Compare how the two writers convey their similar attitudes to crime and punishment.

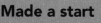

Paper 2, Question 4

For Paper 2, Question 4, you will need to use all your analysis skills to compare the two sources. Look at this worked example, then answer the exam-style question at the bottom of the page.

 Worked example

For this question you will need to refer to the **whole of Source F** on page 96, together with **Source G** on page 97.

Compare how the two writers present their attitudes to employing servants.

In your answer, you could:

- compare their attitudes
- compare the methods they use to convey their attitudes
- support your ideas with references to both texts. **[16 marks]**

Both texts argue that servants are treated unfairly, but they present their ideas in very different ways.

Source F is from the nineteenth century and so has a very serious tone. Formal language such as 'the servant grievance' and 'the increased facilities of locomotion' create an air of authority, making the reader more likely to trust the writer's opinion.

> Start with a clear overview that compares the main ideas and tone of each source. This student identifies a key similarity between the sources, but also acknowledges the differences.

In contrast, the writer of Source G uses colloquial language such as 'lurks' to create a friendly tone that the reader can easily engage with. They also use direct address, encouraging the reader to 'lean in' and hear their secret. This creates a feeling of closeness with the reader, making them more open to agreeing with the writer's point of view.

> For each point, identify **what** choice the writer has made. Explain **how** they have done this, giving evidence from the text. Then, explain **why** you think they have done this, focusing on how it might affect the reader.

Both texts argue that things were better in the past when servants and their employers were more equal. The writer of Source G claims that 'back in the 90s', having an au pair could be a 'win-win situation'. This makes the reader feel more positive about the idea of paying someone to help with the housework.

> Even if you are comparing the writers' ideas, focus on how they are presented and what effect this has on the reader.

Similarly, Source G argues that in the past employers treated their servants much better. She explains that mistresses now are 'unable or unwilling to help them' but that 'It used not to be so.' This short, powerful sentence emphasises how much things have changed.

> Use adverbials, such as 'similarly', to signpost similarities and differences between the sources.

Furthermore, both texts suggest that the middle classes feel housework is beneath them. Source G takes a mocking tone to do this, using a long list to emphasise how many chores they can't do for themselves, such as 'cook, clean, childmind, wash, iron and dog-walk'. However, Source F uses emotive language such as 'seized' and 'frenzy' to highlight how the middle classes' attitudes have changed, suggesting they do not realise the mistakes they are making...

> Use correct subject terminology throughout.

> Draw on all the skills tested in the previous questions. For example, you could write about language, structure or audience and purpose.

 Exam-style practice

For this question, you need to refer to the **whole of Source L** on page 102, together with **Source M** on page 103.

Compare how the two writers convey their different attitudes towards travelling.

In your answer, you could:

- compare their different attitudes
- compare the methods they use to convey their attitudes
- support your ideas with references to both texts. **[16 marks]**

 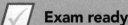

Audience, purpose and form

Paper 1, Question 5 gives you a choice of two descriptive or narrative writing tasks. You will need to show that you can write in a particular form to achieve the purpose of engaging your audience.

② Paper 1, Question 5

This question tests your fiction writing skills. You need to:

- write clearly and effectively, tailoring your language to your audience, purpose and form
- structure your ideas effectively
- use accurate spelling, punctuation and grammar – this is worth 16 of the 40 marks available.

② Purpose

The purpose of your writing will be to write creatively to entertain a particular audience. This will be clear in the question, for example:

> You are going to enter a creative writing competition at your college. The entries will be judged by the headteacher.

② Audience

The audience you should write for will be clear in the question. Possible audiences include:

- ☑ students from your school or college
- ☑ your headteacher
- ☑ adult judges of a competition
- ☑ children at your local primary school.

Choose your language and structure carefully to appeal to your audience. You might use formal, complex language for adults, or punchy, informal language for young people.

② Form

The question will explicitly tell you what form to write in. It could be:

- a short story
- part of a longer story
- a description.

The question will offer you a choice of two tasks. The forms they ask you to write in could be the same or different. If you have a choice of forms, consider which you can write most successfully in.

② Features of narrative

In a narrative you should include:

- ☑ a beginning, a middle and an end (unless the question only asks for part of a narrative, such as an opening)
- ☑ a main character
- ☑ a setting
- ☑ some conflict – this could be dramatic, life-threatening danger, or something as subtle as a mystery or a character's worries
- ☑ a satisfying ending – you could tie up all the loose ends, have a shocking twist, or leave the reader with a cliffhanger. If you are writing just the beginning of a story, the reader should want to read on.

② Features of description

In a description you should:

- ☑ include the five senses to make the reader feel like they are there
- ☑ use figurative language such as similes and metaphors to help the reader picture the scene – go to page 9 to revise this
- ☑ choose your language carefully to have a particular effect on the reader.

⑩ Practice

Write the first paragraph of your answer to this exam-style question, and then annotate it to show how you have tailored your writing to suit the audience, purpose and form.

> You are going to write a story for your school or college magazine.
>
> Your entry will be judged by a panel of students of your own age.
>
> Write a story about a difficult journey.

① Exam focus

In the exam you will only have about 45 minutes to write. If you choose to write a narrative, limit yourself to a few characters and keep the story simple. Focus on the quality of your language and structure.

Vocabulary for effect

In fiction writing, it is important to choose the vocabulary that will have the greatest effect on the reader. Decide what you want the reader to think and feel, then base your choices on these decisions.

② Verbs

Your choice of **verbs** makes a significant contribution to the impact of your writing on the reader. Compare these three examples:

The car <u>drove</u> away, <u>going</u> around the corner and out of sight. Here, the verbs simply describe what happened.

The car <u>screeched</u> away, <u>swerving</u> around the corner and out of sight. Here, 'screeched' suggests danger and panic, and 'swerving' implies that the car is out of control. The reader might imagine a getaway car fleeing the scene of a crime.

The car <u>zoomed</u> away, <u>gliding</u> around the corner and out of sight. Here, 'zoomed' has connotations of speed and power. The verb 'gliding' suggests the car is moving silently and gracefully. Together these verbs suggest skilful driving and a powerful car.

③ Adjectives and adverbs

You can add extra detail to your writing by using **adjectives** to describe nouns and **adverbs** to describe verbs – but be careful not to use too many. Sometimes there is no need for adjectives or adverbs. All the impact you want to create can be achieved with a well chosen noun or verb.

Compare these examples:

The rat ran away.

The horrible, scary rat quickly and quietly ran away.

The rodent scuttled away.

Which version creates the greatest impact?

② Synonyms

Synonyms are words that have the same, or very similar, meaning as each other. For example, synonyms for the word 'big' include mountainous, vast and colossal.

Use synonyms to vary your language and express your ideas precisely.

Always think about which synonym contributes most appropriately and powerfully to your description. Which synonym would you choose to describe a <u>big</u> mountain? Which would you choose to describe a <u>big</u> frightening dog charging towards you?

② Connotations

You can shape the reader's reactions by considering the connotations of the words you choose.

A <u>figure</u> <u>lurked</u> in the <u>dark</u> <u>shadows</u>, beyond the <u>flickering candle</u>. Here, the noun 'figure' is intentionally vague, creating a sense of mystery and danger, while the verb 'lurked' has connotations of secrecy and threat. This feeling is emphasised through the connotations of 'dark' and 'shadows', suggesting something hidden, secret or dangerous, further developed with 'flickering candle' adding to the mood of uncertainty.

② Aiming higher

Think about how your language choices build to create an overall effect. This can be an effective way to create an atmosphere or a tone.

Using language from the semantic field of coldness in a description of a winter scene creates a vivid impression and appeals to the reader's senses. Similarly, focusing your language choices on describing feelings of fear as precisely and powerfully as possible builds a feeling of tension in the reader.

② Patterns

You can use repetition within a sentence to emphasise a key idea, for example:

My life was <u>boring</u>. School was <u>boring</u>, my family were <u>boring</u>, and sometimes even my friends were <u>boring</u>.

This highlights how dull and repetitive the narrator thinks her life is.

You can also use your word choices to create patterns of sound. These can create rhythm and help to engage all the reader's senses. Go to page 6 to revise alliteration, sibilance, assonance and onomatopoeia.

⑩ Practice

Rewrite the narrative extract below, adding, removing and changing words to make it as tense as possible.

> I woke up and sat up. I could hear something moving outside the tent. It was breathing. I was too scared to move, I felt goosebumps on my arms. Then, I picked up my torch and said 'Who's there?'

   Made a start   **Feeling confident**   **Exam ready**

Figurative language for effect

Use figurative language techniques to create vivid imagery and shape your reader's response. Go to page 9 to revise these figurative language techniques.

Metaphors

Use **metaphors** to show how one thing resembles another. This is an effective way to describe without relying on adjectives or adverbs. The connotations of a metaphor can also add another layer of meaning to a description. Metaphors are good for revealing detail about a character or setting, for example:

Armies of holidaymakers marched across the sand.

This metaphor suggests a large crowd of people and the way in which they walk across the sand. However, the connotations of war also suggest that they are disturbing the peace of the beach.

Personification

Personification brings something non-human to life by giving it human qualities. It can be a useful way to bring life to a description.

The morning sun <u>peeped shyly</u> over the edge of the horizon. In this example, the sun is personified as a shy person, suggesting it is slow or reluctant to come up.

Senses

Use figurative language that appeals to the different senses (touch, sight, sound, taste and smell) to immerse your reader more fully in your writing.

For example, using personification to describe the sound of seagulls and wind brings this description to life:

The seagulls screamed and the wind howled as I stepped out onto the cold, wet sand.

Similarly, these metaphors use sensory description to help the reader feel the impact of a strong emotion:

My face burned with humiliation and my pulse thundered in my ears.

Aiming higher

An **extended metaphor** is a metaphor that is continued, for example across two or more sentences. This creates a very strong image for the reader and can be used to emphasise a key idea.

Armies of holidaymakers marched across the sand armed with buckets and spades, quickly invaded the sun beds and marked their territory with towels. Here, the extended army metaphor represents the whole beach as a battlefield. It uses humour to emphasise the impact of these holidaymakers on the peace and quiet of the beach.

Similes

Like metaphors, similes can be used to add detail to a description through their connotations. They are particularly effective as alternatives to adverbs when describing actions, for example:

Tyler crept down the hallway like a <u>panther</u>. Here, the connotations of 'panther' suggest stealth, but also a predator. This makes Tyler's movements seem ominous to the reader.

Figurative language can also be used to help readers build a more vivid impression of characters, for example:

My grandmother's knees <u>creak like rusty hinges</u> when she stands up. This simile describes the unnatural sound the grandmother's knees make. However, 'rust' also has connotations of age and decay, suggesting that her body has been worn out over the years.

Exam focus

The words you choose are as important as the ideas you use in your writing. Try to leave time at the end of the exam to think about the impact of your word choices and consider whether they can be improved.

Practice

Write two paragraphs of your response to this exam-style question, focusing on your use of figurative language.

> You are going to submit a short story for a literature website.
> Your story will be judged by a panel of adult editors.
> Write the opening part of a story about a storm.

Using sentences for effect

In fiction writing, you should structure your sentences carefully to guide the reader through the text and shape their response to it.

② Varying sentence types

Vary the length and form of your sentences to create changes in pace and emphasise key points to the reader. Go to page 10 to revise sentence types.

Connecting many clauses together in a **multi-clause sentence** could suggest a very slow, boring pace:

I gazed at the view out the train window, where nothing much was happening, then I fiddled with my phone, after which I tried to read my book, until finally we were nearly there.

However, it could also create a fast pace where many things happen at once:

Ben knocked the vase, which began to wobble, causing his aunt to shriek, which set off the dog howling.

Single-clause sentences are usually short and simple. You might use one to highlight a particularly important piece of information or to suggest shock:

I couldn't believe it.

A **minor sentence** is even shorter, so can be used to add drama: *Crash!*

Go to pages 77 and 78 for more about beginning and ending sentences effectively.

② Starting a sentence

The way in which you begin a sentence changes its overall tone. For example, an adverb will immediately suggest action:

Silently, I crept towards the door.

A pronoun will focus the reader on a particular character or characters:

He opened the envelope, frowned and then burst out laughing.

An adjective will draw the reader's attention to how something looks, feels, sounds, smells or tastes:

Icy cold air hit my lungs.

② Ending a sentence

In a multi-clause sentence, the information you place at the end usually carries the most weight.

For example: 'I couldn't believe my eyes when I looked up' is less effective than 'When I looked up, I couldn't believe my eyes.' This is because the key idea of the narrator's astonishment gains more emphasis when placed at the end of the sentence.

⑩ Worked example

You are going to submit a piece of creative writing to your school or college website.

Your writing will be judged by a panel of teachers.

Write the opening part of a story about a surprising discovery. **[40 marks]**

...I edged into the room, past crumpled crisp packets, old apple cores and mouldy teacups, then I tiptoed through the broken pieces of one of Mum's best plates before finally reaching a clear patch of floor. Rustling open a bin bag, I lifted the duvet and looked under the bed. I froze. It stared at me from behind a dirty sock. A six-foot snake.

Use a long, multi-clause sentence to build up a detailed picture. Here, the length of the sentence suggests the extent of the mess.

Use minor sentences sparingly to add drama. This sentence focuses all the reader's attention on the snake.

Emphasise important information by putting it at the end of a sentence. Here, 'under the bed' is placed at the end to draw the reader's attention there.

Use contrasts in sentence length to vary the pace and build tension. The short single-clause sentence 'I froze.' is effective because the reader doesn't yet know what the narrator has seen.

Choose the first word of each sentence carefully. Here, 'It' continues to build tension because we don't know what 'It' is.

⑩ Practice

Practise re-writing this paragraph by changing the position of the clauses (you may need to take out some words to avoid repetition). Then add a short sentence to the end of the paragraph.

Made a start | Feeling confident | Exam ready

Paragraphing

Paragraphs organise your writing and make it easier to follow, but they can also be used creatively to have different effects on the reader.

① Organising your writing

You should start a new paragraph when you:
- ☑ move forward or backward in time
- ☑ move to a new setting
- ☑ change character or point of view
- ☑ change topic.

⑩ Worked example

You are going to enter a creative writing competition. Your writing will be judged by a panel of adults. Write a story about a mysterious visitor.

[40 marks]

It started like any other Wednesday night. I was tucked up in bed with a comic and a huge mug of hot chocolate. Rusty, my dog, was curled up contentedly on the floor.

Meanwhile, Dad was ploughing his way through his latest TV obsession downstairs. I listened to the muffled laughter and imagined him stretched out on the sofa, eating crisps and giggling to himself. He deserved a break – he'd been working day and night recently.

Suddenly, there was a knock on the door.

I nearly dropped my hot chocolate with surprise. I paused for a moment, seeing if Dad or Tam would get it, but no such luck. Slowly and painfully, I peeled the duvet off, like it was a plaster.

The knocking became hammering. I shoved my feet into my slippers and dragged myself downstairs, cursing the visitor. With sleepy fingers I pulled back the chain, fumbled with the keys and finally inched open the door. I squinted into the darkness. Slowly, a familiar figure came into focus: my cousin Rachel...

Use very short paragraphs to change the pace of your writing and emphasise key information. This single-sentence paragraph emphasises how the knock on the door disrupts the everyday flow of family life.

⑤ Paragraphs for effect

You can use paragraphing to create an overall effect or atmosphere in your writing. For example, long flowing paragraphs might create a sense of ease and calm to reflect the view on a beautiful train journey. In contrast, short, unlinked paragraphs could help the reader to experience a character's anxiety or tension.

Very short paragraphs, perhaps only one sentence long, can be used to emphasise a key idea or event, for example: Then I saw it. Putting this sentence in a paragraph of its own would create a sense of shock for the reader, as well as building tension while they wait to see what will be revealed in the next paragraph.

Vary the length of your paragraphs to produce changes in pace and tone.

② Linking paragraphs

Link between your paragraphs to connect your ideas and guide the reader through your writing. You can do this by:
- ending a paragraph with a sentence that looks forward to the next paragraph
- starting a new paragraph with a topic sentence or an idea that links back to the previous paragraph
- using adverbial phrases such as 'later', 'after that' and 'yesterday' to help the reader keep track of the action.

These two long, linked paragraphs create a slow, steady pace. This creates a feeling of everyday calm, which might make the reader wonder what is about to happen to disrupt things.

Use adverbial phrases such as 'meanwhile' to link your paragraphs together and guide the reader through your writing.

Think about where you place important information in your paragraphs. Here, withholding the identity of the visitor until the end of the paragraph creates tension for the reader.

⑩ Practice

Write three paragraphs of your own in response to the exam-style question above, thinking about the structure of your paragraphs.

 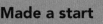 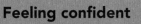

Creative openings

The opening of your narrative or descriptive writing needs to engage your reader as quickly as possible. In the opening of a piece of descriptive writing, you could choose to create a sense of mystery, or begin with a vivid **description** of place. You can do both of these in the opening of a piece of narrative writing, or choose to use **dialogue** or **conflict** to engage your reader.

Dialogue

Starting with dialogue throws your reader into the middle of a conversation and gives them an immediate impression of the characters who are speaking.

'It's all my fault! I should have minded my own business.' whispered Ivy, her voice shaking.

Nisha blinked the tears out of her eyes and fiercely grabbed her friend's hand.

'It's OK – you couldn't have known. All that matters now is getting out of here.' Her words came out so bravely that she almost believed they could make it.

From this opening, the reader can infer that Ivy feels guilty and afraid, Nisha is trying to be strong, and the girls are in a dangerous situation. The reader immediately feels the tension of the situation.

Conflict

You could start your writing in the middle of the action by plunging your reader straight into a moment of conflict or danger. This would work well for part of a longer story.

I waited. In the distance I could just hear the rumble of a tram passing the end of the road. Nothing could be seen in the pitch black cellar and all I could feel was the rise and fall of my chest as I tried to keep my breathing under control.

In this example, the uncertainty about what is happening guides the reader to share in the narrator's fear and tension.

 Mystery

Beginning with a mystery poses questions in the reader's mind, making them want to read on and find out the answers. It can be an effective way to draw the reader into a piece of descriptive writing.

I'll never forget the first time I saw the old house.

Here, the reader doesn't know anything about the house, only that it is significant. This engages their curiosity and makes them want to know more.

If the purpose of your writing is to describe, limit the amount of dialogue you use as it may detract from your descriptive techniques.

 Description

Beginning with a detailed description is an effective way to immerse your reader in a particular setting or atmosphere. This is a good opportunity to show off your vocabulary and figurative language skills if you are writing a narrative.

No one knew how long the house had stood there. The green paint on its front door had faded to a sad grey, and torn, dirty curtains flapped forlornly in the windows. Tear stains of damp streaked its walls.

This description conveys a strong atmosphere of sadness and decay, setting the tone and engaging the reader's emotions.

Exam focus

Think carefully about your audience, purpose and subject matter when choosing your opening. For example, beginning with conflict or mystery would be suitable for an exciting story for young people.

Practice

Write the opening two paragraphs of your response to this exam-style question.

You are going to enter a creative writing competition.

Your entry will be judged by a panel of people your own age.

Write a description suggested by this picture:

Creative endings

The ending is the part of your writing that the reader will remember most. Whether you are writing a description, a short story or part of a longer story, make sure you include an effective ending.

② Resolution

Resolving conflict is a satisfying way to end a short story. You can do this by showing how the characters have changed or learned from their mistakes.

Later, everybody wondered what all the fuss had been about. Nobody was hurt, nobody had died. But Ali would never forget that moment of panic. He reached for his little sister's hand and clutched it tightly. He would never let it go again.

This ending shows that Ali has learned from his experiences and will look after his sister more carefully in the future.

① Exam focus

Spend a few minutes planning before you start writing. Make sure you leave enough time to include an effective ending, as a clear and complete resolution is an important element of the creative writing tasks.

② A cliffhanger

A cliffhanger leaves the reader with unanswered questions. It is a good way to end a section of a longer story or add a little drama to a description. However, make sure it fits with the overall tone.

This example is an interesting way to end a description of a woodland:

Sunlight streamed through the trees, their shadows gently swaying in the breeze, and the birds sang loudly and happily. A blackbird landed on the ground and pulled up a worm.

Suddenly I knew what I had to do. I was going to stand up for myself once and for all.

The cliffhanger suggests that the beautiful setting has given the narrator inspiration to take action about something. This captures the reader's imagination and makes them wonder what might happen.

⑤ A twist

A twist allows you to end a story on a surprising, funny or shocking note. In a narrative, you could reveal something that changes everything for the characters. Alternatively, you could end a description with an unexpected change in atmosphere. Keep your twist simple and make sure it fits with your audience and purpose.

I tried to breathe slowly and move past my fear. I couldn't stop my hand from shaking as I stretched my trembling fingers towards the door. Then, in one desperate movement, I grabbed the handle and twisted it open.

A pair of glowing eyes loomed out of the darkness. Claws skittered and scratched on the floor. A strange musty smell invaded my nose. I shoved my hand over my mouth to crush a scream.

Barry, my dog, bounded through the door, howling for joy, and planted a big wet kiss on my face.

This twist changes the whole feel of the narrative, taking the reader on a funny and exciting emotional journey.

⑤ Cyclical structure

A cyclical structure brings the reader back round to where they began, making your writing feel complete and satisfying. You could echo something that is said at the beginning, or focus your ending on the place, person or object you started with.

It is a particularly good way to end descriptive writing as it gives your writing a sense of overall direction and structure.

Lying in bed, anxious and uncomfortable, I watched the sun slowly fill the sky with colour. The whole world was fast asleep. Except me.

...

I pulled open the curtains and climbed into bed. Exhausted but happy, I fell asleep in the silver light of a huge full moon.

⑩ Practice

Write the last two paragraphs of your response to this exam-style question.

> You are going to write a short story for your school or college magazine.
>
> Your entry will be judged by a panel of students.
>
> Write a story about bravery.

 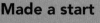

Implying meaning

Implying meaning is an effective way to engage your reader's interest and add depth to characters and settings.

② Implicit information

You don't have to explicitly tell the reader everything you want them to know about a character or setting. It is far more effective to focus on specific details that create the impression you want to make.

For example, there is no need to tell the reader that the narrator's sister is very angry with him in this story opening: My sister slammed the front door and stormed up the stairs to my room like an unstoppable hurricane.

Similarly, there is no need to tell the reader in this story opening that the action takes place outside on a beautiful summer's day: The sun beat down and a gentle breeze rustled the leaves of the trees.

⑩ Worked example

You are going to submit a piece of creative writing to your local newspaper.

Your writing will be judged by a panel of adults.

Write the opening of a story about school.

[40 marks]

Outside, dark clouds loomed on the horizon and the wind slapped wet leaves against the window. A sudden burst of rain hit the windows and trickled miserably down the glass. Trapped inside by the awful weather, we slouched behind our desks, heads bent over mobiles, our fingers racing.

Nobody even spoke until Tom found the football. For a few minutes, he just kept bouncing it off one foot. It was only when the girls started shouting his name and cheering that he moved out of his chair. His hair actually brushed the classroom ceiling when he headed the ball. Hours of practice with the school team paid off as it sailed across the room and hit me hard in the face. Black dots danced in front of my eyes as I struggled to stay upright. Tom laughed...

Plan when and where to reveal clues. In this example, the writer only implies the unpleasant side of Tom's character at the very end. This takes the reader on an interesting emotional journey – their admiration of Tom might turn into disapproval.

Show, don't tell. This description expressively captures the narrator's experience of dizziness, guiding the reader to sympathise.

Use the description of the setting to imply an atmosphere or foreshadow what is to come.

② Creating setting

Use descriptions of setting to help create the mood you want to achieve in your writing. You could:

- use descriptions of the weather to create an atmosphere that suggests how a story will develop or to reflect the feelings of a character (pathetic fallacy). For example, a storm could suggest that dangerous or dramatic events will take place, or reflect a character's feelings of anger or despair.

- focus on specific details of a building or location. For example, broken windows and an overgrown garden immediately suggest a derelict or uninhabited house, and create a sense of mystery and danger.

② Creating character

Rather than telling the reader what a character is like, choose descriptive detail that reveals something about their personality or emotional state. We get to know people through facial expressions and body language, so make use of these details to imply what characters are thinking and feeling, and bring them to life for the reader. Look at these examples:

Mike <u>leapt</u> through the puddles. Here, 'leapt' suggests joy, creating an impression of Mike as happy and carefree.

Kayla <u>stamped</u> through the puddles. 'Stamped' suggests anger, creating an impression of Kayla as frustrated or unhappy.

Figurative language can imply information more strongly:

Mike leapt over the puddles like a dancer.

Kayla was a terrifying monster, stamping through the puddles.

Leave clues about characters' personalities. This description implies that Tom is tall, handsome, good at football and popular with the girls.

⑩ Practice

Write the opening three paragraphs of your response to this exam-style question. Focus on implying meaning to the reader.

You are going to enter a creative writing competition.

Your entry will be judged by teachers from your school or college.

Write the opening part of a story about telling a lie.

✓ **Made a start** ✓ **Feeling confident** ✓ **Exam ready**

Gathering descriptive ideas

Before you start writing a description, it is a good idea to gather and organise your ideas. This will help you to structure your writing effectively.

 Picture the scene

One way to gather ideas for a descriptive writing task is to picture yourself inside the scene. Ask these questions:

- Who else is here?
- Who am I and why am I here?
- What emotions do I feel?
- What is just out of sight?
- What can I see, hear, smell, touch and taste?

Organise your ideas

Spending a few minutes jotting down your ideas will help you to organise them. A spider diagram is a good way to survey your ideas quickly and see how they could connect and develop.

Make a note of as many ideas as you can, then look back over them, circling or ticking the most effective ones. Go to page 56 to read more about structuring descriptive writing.

Use questions to come up with your key ideas. Include any ideas for interesting vocabulary or figurative language.

 Worked example

You are going to submit a piece of creative writing to your school or college website.

Your writing will be judged by your headteacher.

Write a description suggested by this picture:

[40 marks]

Add extra branches to develop and link your ideas. Here, sounds and smells have been combined into an idea for an extended metaphor.

✓ 'a monster's den' – extended metaphor?

✓ hear 'roaring' trains 'like dragons' ← Senses? → ✓ smell dust and dirt – smell 'creeps' and 'lurks'

feel cold, slippery tiles – take small, uncertain steps

Who else? ✓ strange adults, 'dull clothing', 'stony faces', a 'herd'

Train station

Out of sight? worried family

Emotions? ✓ fear, isolation, intimidated by strangers

Who? ✓ small boy, lost

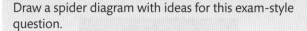 **Practice**

Draw a spider diagram with ideas for this exam-style question.

You are going to enter a creative writing competition.

Your entry will be judged by a panel of people of your own age.

Write a description suggested by this picture:

Structuring descriptive writing

You need to structure your descriptive writing carefully to guide the reader through the scene. This will help you to shape what they think and feel as they read.

② Structuring a description

When you have gathered your ideas, write a brief plan to structure them. Description can be structured in a similar way to narrative writing, but be sure to focus on description rather than on telling a story. Your description could include:

- ☑ an engaging opening (go to page 52)
- ☑ a middle, including a simple conflict or climax. You could draw the reader's attention to a significant element in the scene, or develop the narrator's thoughts or feelings. You could also include hints about what events have led up to this point.
- ☑ a satisfying ending, such as a cliffhanger or a return to the beginning (go to page 53).

⑩ Worked example

You are going to enter a creative writing competition.

Your entry will be judged by a panel of people your own age.

Write a description suggested by this picture:

<u>Beginning</u> **[40 marks]**

- Dramatic first sentence – 'I'm all alone.'
- Detailed description of crowds rushing past. Child's perspective – focus on legs and feet ('herds', 'dull clothing'), move up to 'stony faces'.
- Sense of panic – heat rising up from the pit of my stomach. Eyes 'drowning' in tears.

<u>Middle</u>

- Senses – trains 'roaring like dragons', dirt and dust 'creeps' and 'lurks'. Extended metaphor – 'a monster's den'.
- Zoom in on sister's rucksack, just moving out of sight on escalator. 'A gleam of hope'.
- Panning, follow boy running, past crowds. Breath burns in lungs. Must escape monster!

<u>End</u>

- Make it up escalator – family waiting at top. Relieved but proud – feel like I've defeated a hundred monsters.

② Narrative perspective

It is important to think about what you show the reader, when you show it to them, and how you show it to them. You may want to focus the reader's attention gradually on an important or unusual object. For example, an abandoned mobile phone ringing in a beautiful woodland scene would create a sense of mystery.

Think about the order in which you reveal information. Withholding something significant until the end is an effective way to introduce a twist, while slowly revealing clues about something will build tension.

Go to page 20 to revise narrative perspective.

⑤ Cinematic techniques

A helpful way to think about structure is to imagine yourself as a film director in charge of a camera.

- Zoom in on an important object or person to draw the reader's attention. This could be used to create a feeling of mystery or imply a backstory.
- Pan 360° to give the reader an overview of the scene and help them feel as though they are there.
- Track the narrator or another character through the scene. This develops the reader's relationship with them and creates a sense of discovery when new features are revealed.
- Give a bird's eye view to create distance, guiding the reader to see a scene in a new or unusual way. For example, a city might look like a machine, suggesting how mechanical and busy life is there.

⑩ Practice

Plan your response to this exam-style question.

You are going to enter a creative writing competition.

Your entry will be judged by a panel of people of your own age.

Write a description suggested by this picture:

Gathering narrative ideas

Before you start writing a narrative, it is a good idea to gather and organise your ideas. This will help you to structure your writing effectively.

① Character

Focus on just one or two main characters. Ask yourself these questions:

Who are they?

What are they like?

What emotions do they feel?

How should the reader feel about them?

② Setting and atmosphere

Setting and atmosphere are valuable ways to quickly make a strong impact on the reader. Think about the language you could use to emphasise a particular atmosphere. For example, in a dark room you might focus on sounds to build tension and mystery.

Consider whether your setting has any connotations that imply additional meaning. For example, an abandoned castle might have frightening connotations of violence and war. Go to pages 25–26 to revise setting and atmosphere.

② Plot and genre

Begin to plan by deciding which genre or type of story you want to write and the impact you want it to have on your reader, for example, a thrilling mystery or an exciting adventure. You can then start building your plot. Your plot should be short and simple. Think about what emotions you want the reader to feel and what type of story you want to write. Narrative writing needs:

- an engaging opening to grab the reader's attention (go to page 52)
- a middle including a simple conflict or climax
- a satisfying ending, such as a cliffhanger, a twist or a return to the beginning (go to page 53).

Go to page 58 to revise how to structure narrative writing.

② Narrative voice

Your choice of narrative voice can greatly change the tone of your narrative. For example, a first person voice will help you to develop the main character and build a personal relationship with the reader. An omniscient third person voice is effective if you want to give the reader a detailed, unbiased understanding of events.

Go to page 24 to revise narrative voice.

⑩ Worked example

You are going to enter a creative writing competition.

Your writing will be judged by a panel of young people.

Write a story about a mysterious visitor. **[40 marks]**

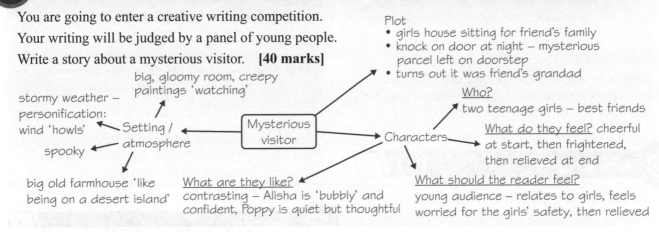

big, gloomy room, creepy paintings 'watching'

stormy weather – personification: wind 'howls'

spooky

Setting / atmosphere

big old farmhouse 'like being on a desert island'

Mysterious visitor

Plot
- girls house sitting for friend's family
- knock on door at night – mysterious parcel left on doorstep
- turns out it was friend's grandad

Who? two teenage girls – best friends

What do they feel? cheerful at start, then frightened, then relieved at end

Characters

What are they like? contrasting – Alisha is 'bubbly' and confident, Poppy is quiet but thoughtful

What should the reader feel? young audience – relates to girls, feels worried for the girls' safety, then relieved

⑩ Practice

Draw a spider diagram with ideas for your response to this exam-style question.

You are going to submit a piece of creative writing to your local newspaper.

Your writing will be judged by a panel of adults.

Write a story about a surprise.

Structuring narrative writing

Use structure in your narrative writing to shape the reader's response and take them on a journey. A four-part structure is an effective way to do this.

(5) The four-part story

If you are writing a whole story, this four-part structure will help you to guide the reader effectively. If you are writing part of a story, you might focus on two of the boxes. For example, the opening to a story might cover the exposition and main event. However, you should still aim to include an engaging ending such as a cliffhanger to make the reader want to find out what happens next.

1. Exposition
The characters and setting are introduced and described.

2. Main event
Something happens or begins to go wrong. This is often where suspense is created.

3. Development
The characters respond to what has happened. This is often the high point of tension.

4. Resolution
Conflicts are resolved and loose ends are tied up.

(10) Worked example

You are going to enter a creative writing competition. Your writing will be judged by a panel of young people.

Write a story about a mysterious visitor.

[40 marks]

<u>1. Exposition</u>

Two friends are home alone in a farmhouse on a dark and stormy night.

<u>2. Main event</u>

Knock on door frightens girls. Nobody there but package left on step – suspense.

<u>3. Development</u>

The girls argue about whether to open package. They decide to wait until daylight. Have sleepless night.

<u>4. Resolution</u>

Wake up to a sunny morning. They open the package and find chocolates and DVDs from friend's grandad as a thank-you for looking after the house.

(2) Aiming higher ⬆

Experiment with the four-part story structure. Try starting with the main event and then flashing back to the exposition, or starting with the resolution. This story begins with the ending:

Source – The Five People You Meet in Heaven

This is a story about a man named Eddie and it begins at the end, with Eddie dying in the sun. It might seem strange to start a story with an ending. But all endings are also beginnings. We just don't know it at the time.

(2) Narrative perspective

You also need to consider how to guide the reader's attention through the narrative. Imagine you are a film director in charge of a camera.

For example, you could withhold an important element to create a feeling of mystery and suspense. Alternatively, you could repeatedly show the reader an object, a character or an idea to highlight its significance. Shifts in perspective can also be used to signal a change in mood or atmosphere.

Go to page 20 to revise narrative perspective.

Stick to one or two characters and describe them in more detail.

Choose a simple main event that creates tension but can be described clearly. An argument, a surprising phone call or an amusing mistake is enough.

Focus on creating tension in the story's development. Withholding a key piece of information is a good way to do this. In this example, the source and contents of the parcel are left a mystery.

Choose an ending that finishes the story in a satisfying way. Usually, the reader will want a resolution to the tension built up in the development section.

(10) Practice

Plan your response to this exam-style question.

You are going to submit a piece of creative writing to your local newspaper.

Your writing will be judged by a panel of adults.

Write a story about a surprise.

Narrative writing

One or both of the options in Paper 1, Question 5 could be a narrative writing task. Look at this worked example and then try the exam-style practice.

 Worked example

You are going to enter a creative writing competition. Your entry will be judged by a panel of students from your school or college.

Write the opening part of a story about a family holiday.

(24 marks for content and organisation

16 marks for technical accuracy)

[40 marks]

I awoke with a start. Something wasn't right.

It wasn't just my sister breathing her horrible dog-breath into my face. It wasn't the mind-numbing sound of the endless rain drumming on the canvas. It wasn't even being trapped on this stupid camping holiday.

Drip. Drop. Drip. Drop.

A huge raindrop slowly grew on the roof of the tent, hung there impossibly for a moment like a big, fat Christmas bauble, and then plummeted, splashing me right on the nose. Great. Irritably, I sat up and grabbed my glasses, which just happened to be floating past. I shook the water off and jammed them on my face.

That's when it hit me. All our stuff – my makeup bag, Lisa's felt tips, a bag of weird French sweets – was floating! I gazed around the tent in amazement, giggling at a saucepan bobbing around like a toy boat in a bath.

Finally, the cold seeping through my sleeping bag shocked me to my senses. The tent was flooding – I had to do something!

Instinctively, I groped for my phone, which was lurking in murky water. With numb fingers I jabbed desperately at the power button. It flickered for a moment, made a sad little noise and then went blank.

I spotted my trainers drifting near Lisa's favourite toy bear. I grabbed the laces and towed them towards me, then screamed as a huge, glistening frog leapt out of one.

I'm a great believer in expecting the worst – that way, things don't usually turn out so badly. However, even my gloomiest imaginings couldn't have prepared me for the scene awaiting me when I unzipped the tent...

Both options for Paper 1, Question 5 include 16 marks for accurate spelling, punctuation and grammar.

Use your opening to create an instant impact on the reader. This very short opening paragraph creates tension by throwing the reader straight into a tense situation.

Use minor sentences to add drama and vary the pace of your writing. Here, they add sound to the scene, but also imply something about the narrator's situation.

Use figurative language such as similes to help the reader imagine the scene. This metaphor creates a surreal image that reflects the strangeness of the situation.

Choose precise verbs to bring the action to life for the reader. In this example, 'jammed' implies the narrator's grumpy mood and carelessness.

Vary your vocabulary, but be cautious with ambitious words – only use them if they contribute to the effect and you are sure of their meaning.

Use your ending to make a final impact on the reader. This writing task asked for the opening of a story, so a cliffhanger is an effective way to round off the section and leave the reader wanting more.

 Exam-style practice

You are going to submit a piece of creative writing to your school or college magazine.

Your entry will be judged by a panel of students.

Write the opening part of a story about a mysterious event. **[40 marks]**

Descriptive writing

One or both of the options in Paper 1, Question 5 could be a descriptive writing task. Look at this worked example and then try the exam-style practice.

 Worked example ✓

You are going to enter a creative writing competition. Your entry will be judged by a panel of students.

Write a description suggested by this picture:

(24 marks for content and organisation
16 marks for technical accuracy)

[40 marks]

Warm sunshine flooded the room as Alice pulled back the curtains. She stood silently for a moment drinking in the view. Blue sky and soft golden sand beckoned her down to the sea, which sparkled in the early morning sun. Alice dropped her book, towel and sun cream into her beloved old beach bag, and slung it over her shoulder.

Throwing open the door, she drew in a deep, contented breath. The fresh, clean sea air filled her body, energising her. Warm sand spilled over her sandals, gently tickling her toes. In the distance, the waves sang their familiar whispering song, inviting her to dive right in. Part of her wanted to charge down to the sea, laughing and shouting, but instead she gently strolled. Some moments deserved to be savoured.

She wandered past spiky clumps of dune grass and tiny, hopping, sand-coloured birds, cheerily going about their day. It was a perfect morning. But she knew the peace would only last so long.

Soon, armies of sunbathers would appear and invade the beach. Beach towels, colourful umbrellas and packed lunches would cover the sand, marking out territory. The noise of children playing and adults chatting would fill the air...

She closed her eyes. The sea softly slid over her feet, and the sun smiled on her face.

For a few hours, the beach was just for her.

End your description in a satisfying way. Here, the ending takes the reader back to the peace described at the start.

The picture provided is just a starting point. You can describe extra features, or imagine what is just outside the scene.

Both options for Paper 1, Question 5 include 16 marks for accurate spelling, punctuation and grammar.

Choose your language carefully. Here, the unusual verb 'drinking' effectively captures Alice's pleasure at the scene.

Use cinematic techniques to guide the reader through the scene. Here, the narrative focus tracks Alice as she walks towards the sea. This helps the reader to imagine that they too are walking on the beach.

Think about all five senses. Here, 'sang' adds a gentle sound to the reader's picture of the scene.

Include an element of tension or conflict to give your description a sense of shape and structure.

Vary the length of your sentences. This short sentence slows the reader's pace, matching Alice's movements.

 Exam-style practice ✓

You are going to enter a creative writing competition. Your entry will be judged by a panel of adults.

Write a description suggested by this picture:

[40 marks]

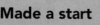 **Made a start** **Feeling confident** **Exam ready**

Audience, form and purpose

Paper 2, Question 5 is a non-fiction writing task. You will need to show that you can write in a particular form for a specific audience in order to achieve the purpose of presenting a point of view.

② Paper 2, Question 5

This question tests your non-fiction writing skills, but has the same assessment objectives as Paper 1, Question 5. You will need to:

- write clearly and effectively, tailoring your language to your audience, purpose and form
- structure your ideas carefully
- use accurate spelling, punctuation and grammar – this is worth 16 of the 40 marks available.

① Exam focus

Choose your language to suit your form, audience and purpose. An audience of young people might prefer an informal approach, but you might avoid using colloquialisms if you are writing for your school or college newspaper.

⑩ Form

Different forms of writing are used for different purposes.

① An **article** might be used to argue your point of view or explain about a topic (go to page 69).

② A **letter** can be used to persuade or argue your point to a particular audience (go to page 70). The audience of this letter would be the headteacher of your school.

③ A **speech** is a persuasive piece of writing intended to be spoken out loud. The audience could be your class, your teachers or a group of strangers (go to page 71).

④ An **essay** is a piece of writing presenting your point of view in response to a statement. It should use formal language and a serious tone (go to page 72).

⑤ A **leaflet** might be used to advertise or instruct (go to page 73). This leaflet is a guide to recycling, so it might be simply informative or it might be trying to persuade people to recycle more.

① Rethinking Recycling

② Dear Mrs Greenfield, I am writing to you about our school's recycling policy...

③

④ The UK throws away over 1 million tonnes of plastic each year, most of which could be easily recycled.

⑤

② Your point of view

Your purpose in this task is to present a viewpoint. Pages 62–68 cover techniques that help you to do this. The task could ask you to explain, argue or persuade the reader to agree with your point of view. To achieve any of these successfully, you first need to decide on your point of view. Read the statement in the question carefully and underline the key words. Then, consider your opinion – do you agree or disagree, and why?

This statement is negative about our treatment of the environment.

> 'We are <u>destroying</u> the <u>environment</u>. It's <u>our duty</u> to do something before it is too late.'
>
> Write an article for your college newspaper in which you explain your point of view on this statement.

The topic is the environment.

The focus is on our responsibility to protect the environment.

⑩ Practice

Write the first paragraph of your response to this exam-style question, and then annotate it to show how you have tailored your writing to suit your audience, purpose and form.

> 'Healthy eating is the key to living a long and happy life. We must educate young people so that they make healthier food choices.'
>
> Write a letter to your headteacher in which you explain your point of view on this statement.

Writing for an audience

The audience is the person or people you are writing for. In Paper 2, Question 5, you will need to tailor your language to a particular audience.

 Choosing appropriate language

Customers: you might be asked to write a leaflet advertising a product. To persuade the reader, you could use short, punchy sentences and alliteration to make your writing memorable.

Your class: you could be asked to write a speech arguing your point of view to your class or school. For this audience, make sure you use rhetorical techniques and informal or colloquial language to engage them.

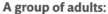
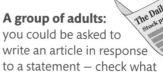
examples of target audiences

A professional adult: you might be asked to write a letter to your local MP or your headteacher. For this audience, you should write in Standard English and use a formal tone and sophisticated vocabulary to make your writing sound mature.

A group of adults: you could be asked to write an article in response to a statement — check what sort of publication it's for. If you think it should be more formal, for example for a broadsheet newspaper, use specialised vocabulary, facts and statistics and complex sentence forms to make your writing sound persuasive and professional (go to page 69 for the difference between a tabloid and a broadsheet newspaper).

A group of young people: the question might ask you to write an article for your school newspaper. This implies that your audience is people your age. Although you should generally use Standard English, you can also include some more informal features to engage them: contractions, rhetorical devices, and colloquial and informal language, if appropriate.

 Worked example

'The internet has transformed the way we work, rest and play. It has changed our lives for the better.'
Write an article for a broadsheet newspaper in which you explain your point of view on this statement.

[40 marks]

The internet has undoubtedly transformed our lives in many positive ways. We are better connected, have limitless information at our fingertips and can buy just about anything at the click of a button.

However, this comes at a price. We're constantly bombarded with texts, emails, news and information from morning till night. Even worse, young people are growing up facing greater and greater social pressures online; while parents barely understand these pressures, they have no hope of protecting their children from them...

A broadsheet newspaper article should be formal and serious, whereas a tabloid article can be more informal and dramatic. Go to page 69 to revise types of articles.

Use sophisticated language such as 'undoubtedly' when writing for an adult audience.

Give examples that your audience will be able to relate to. Here, work and children are concerns that will be of interest to adults.

Use complex sentence structures to engage an adult audience.

 Practice

Choose a paragraph from a broadsheet newspaper and rewrite it for a teenage audience.

Introductions

In non-fiction writing, your opening should not only outline your viewpoint but also engage your audience. Using one or two of the techniques below will help you to write an effective introduction.

A statement

You can begin with a bold or controversial statement to shock the reader and grab their attention.

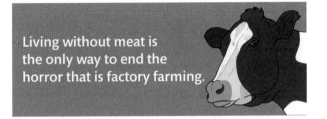

Living without meat is the only way to end the horror that is factory farming.

A rhetorical question

A rhetorical question guides the reader to think about their own opinions, helping them to engage with your topic.

Have you ever stopped to consider the life lived by the chicken on your plate?

An anecdote

An anecdote is a short story from your own experience or from the experience of someone you know. It can be used to create human interest and quickly build a strong relationship with the reader.

The first time I saw my uncle's chicken farm was the last time I ever ate meat!

This anecdote is engaging because it makes the reader want to know why the experience so strongly affected the writer.

A fact or statistic

You could begin with a dramatic piece of information to shock the reader and secure their attention.

70% of the chickens you eat never set foot outside a cage.

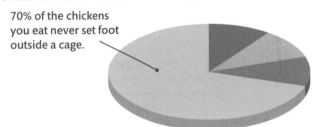

In the exam, you can make up facts and statistics. However, make sure they sound believable.

'Factory farming is often criticised, but it is the only option if the population continues to grow at its present rate.'

Write an article for a broadsheet newspaper in which you explain your point of view on this statement.

[40 marks]

We eat 2.2 million chickens every day in the UK. The majority will have spent their entire lives in a tiny cage before being crammed into a wooden crate and taken to the slaughterhouse. Factory farming might be feeding the nation, but we must consider alternatives to this awful animal cruelty...

Grab the reader's attention in your first sentence. This example uses a shocking statistic.

Use the rest of your first paragraph to give a brief overview of your opinion. This example makes it clear that the writer opposes factory farming.

Choose your language carefully to develop the reader's emotional response. Here, the emotive words 'crammed' and 'slaughterhouse' make the reader feel sorry for the chickens.

Write two different opening paragraphs in response to this exam-style question, using the techniques on this page.

'Young people need to be more involved in politics. The voting age should be lowered to 16, and voting should be made compulsory for everyone under 18.'

Write an article for a tabloid newspaper in which you explain your point of view on this statement.

Conclusions

In non-fiction writing, you need a strong conclusion to leave the reader with a lasting message. Using one of the methods below will help you to write an effective ending.

 Ideas for conclusions

A vivid image

Ending with a striking image will leave a memorable picture in the reader's mind. This can be used to develop a strong emotion such as anger or guilt.

> Next time you're tempted to spend the day on the sofa, just imagine your poor muscles shrinking and shrivelling.

This gruesome image will stick in the reader's mind and make them think about the consequences of not exercising.

A question

A question will prompt the reader to keep thinking about your point of view after they have finished reading about it.

> We should all be asking ourselves, is that TV boxset really more important than our health?

A positive note

Ending on a positive note will leave the reader feeling inspired and optimistic, which might prompt them to take action.

> Now is our chance to make a difference. By making a few simple changes now we can change the future for generations to come.

A warning

Outline the consequences of not taking action to alarm the reader into considering your point of view.

> If we continue with our lazy ways, **obesity** and **heart disease** will affect **over 40%** of the population **by 2030**.

This warning about obesity and heart disease prompts the reader to consider the risks of not exercising and may encourage them to change their ways.

A call to action

A call to action might use rousing **imperative verbs** to motivate the reader to act.

> So grab your trainers and get active!

 Exam focus

Even if you are running out of time, make sure you spend a few minutes writing a strong conclusion.

 Aiming higher

Consider using a cyclical structure to link your ending back to the beginning. This can be particularly effective if you started with an anecdote, for example:

> My uncle has always been quite unhealthy, but it didn't seem a big deal. Until he had a heart attack at just 40 years old. He made a full recovery, but I'll never forget the fear of losing him...

> Of course there are cold, rainy days when all I want to do is slump on the sofa with a pizza. But then I think of my uncle in that hospital bed, and suddenly going for a run doesn't seem so bad after all.

Practice

Write two different concluding paragraphs in response to this exam-style question, using the techniques on this page.

> 'Young people need to be more involved in politics. The voting age should be lowered to 16, and voting should be made compulsory for everyone under 18.'
>
> Write an article for a tabloid newspaper in which you explain your point of view on this statement.

 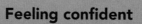

Directing the reader

In order to be persuasive, your writing needs to be easy for the reader to follow. Use paragraphs and linking features to guide them through your argument.

⏱ Paragraphs

Break down your argument for the reader by starting a new paragraph for each new point you make.

Your paragraphs should be structured to make your points effectively. In each paragraph you should:

- begin with a **topic sentence** – a sentence that clearly introduces the main point of the paragraph or links back to the previous paragraph:

  Fossil fuels such as coal and gas are not going to last forever.

  Homework puts an enormous amount of pressure on students.

- develop the main point by explaining it in more detail and making any related points
- support your point with evidence, if appropriate.

⏱ Worked example

'Factory farming is often criticised, but it is the only option if the population continues to grow at its present rate.'

Write an article for a broadsheet newspaper in which you explain your point of view on this statement.

[40 marks]

It is wrong to ignore cruelty. Some might argue that an animal's life is not as important as a human's. In fact, they may even argue that some animals exist only as food for us. However, this is no excuse for the cruelty that some animals suffer. For example, 95% of the chickens that end up on our plates have never walked in the fresh air.

Animal cruelty is just one of the reasons why we should consider alternatives to factory farming. Our health is another. We don't need to eat meat to have a healthy diet. There are lots of good sources of protein: beans, nuts and lentils. Nuts are also a great source of important vitamins. Furthermore, fresh fruit and vegetables are a valuable source of fibre, so we would all benefit from eating more of them...

⏱ Linking your ideas

Use adverbials to make connections between your ideas and signpost the direction of your argument.

Purpose	Examples
Adding an idea	in addition, furthermore
Explaining a result	therefore, consequently
Illustrating an idea	for example, for instance
Emphasising an idea	significantly, in particular
Comparing ideas	similarly, likewise
Contrasting ideas	however, on the other hand

For example:

There are many alternatives to fossil fuels, for instance...

Your ideas should be linked together so that the reader's thoughts and feelings change as they read. Go to page 75 to revise structuring non-fiction.

Start each paragraph with a topic sentence to introduce its main point or purpose.

Use adverbials to draw attention to key points in each paragraph. In this example, 'in fact' emphasises the statement that some people think that animals are only food, making it seem more shocking.

Next, develop your point. Here, a counterargument and statistic are used to support the idea that factory farming is wrong.

Make clear links between your paragraphs. This paragraph refers back to the previous one and explains how it will follow on.

Use a range of punctuation accurately to express your view clearly.

Use adverbials to connect ideas. The adverbial 'furthermore' indicates that the writer is going to add another similar idea. It creates the impression that the writer has lots of points in support of their argument.

⏱ Practice

Write three paragraphs of your response to this exam-style question, focusing on directing the reader.

'Computer games are too violent. They set a bad example for children and encourage bad behaviour.'
Write an article for a tabloid newspaper in which you explain your point of view on this statement.

Influencing the reader

Use language, sentence structure and evidence carefully to create a deliberate effect on the reader.

 ② Sentence structure

Think carefully about your choice of sentence forms (go to page 50).

Multi-clause sentences create a fluid, sophisticated tone: *While cycling has been enjoyed in the UK since the Victorian times, it has soared in popularity in the past twenty years – largely due to significant investment.*

Single-clause sentences are easy to follow and draw attention to a key point: *We are destroying the planet.*

Minor sentences can be used occasionally to add emphasis or drama: *I have at least three hours of homework a night. Every night.*

⑤ Worked example

'Our nation is losing its sense of community. Volunteering should be a compulsory part of the school curriculum.'

Write a speech to be given at your school or college in which you explain your point of view on this statement. **[40 marks]**

Education isn't all about grades – it's about becoming an adult. This is why I believe that volunteering should be added to the school curriculum.

Modern life is cutting us off from our community. We are robots, mechanically marching past homeless people in the street, too busy and distracted to notice them. Even calling our own grandparents seems like a chore. Things have to change.

A recent study found that almost three-quarters of older people in the UK feel lonely. Just think what a difference we could make if we each took just one hour away from our textbooks to reach out to these vulnerable people...

Use evidence to support some of your points and make your argument sound believable.

② Figurative language

Use figurative language to create a striking image, in order to emphasise an emotion or a key point (go to page 49).

In rush hour, passengers are crammed onto the buses like cattle. Here, a simile highlights the crowding and implies that the passengers are treated like animals.

Homework is a ball and chain around the ankles of every child in the nation. This emotive metaphor emphasises how great a burden homework is. Its connotations also imply that students feel like they are being unfairly punished.

 ② Vocabulary

Vocabulary choice can help you to create a particular tone or style to guide the reader's response (go to page 48). In an essay, you could use sophisticated and technical language to create a serious, professional tone: *Carbon emissions must be significantly reduced.*

In an article, you could use energetic verbs to create a lively, inspiring tone: *The feeling of gliding along country lanes and racing down hills is like nothing else.*

② Evidence

Use evidence to support your point of view. This suggests that you are knowledgeable about your topic and that your ideas are reasonable. In the exam, you can make up evidence as long as it is believable. You could use expert opinions, statistics, facts or anecdotes.

Be careful not to overuse evidence. A few striking examples will be most effective.

Use figurative language to create a strong emotion in the reader. This metaphor implies that people are cold and emotionless.

Vary your sentence structure for effect. This short sentence stands out and signals a shift from explaining the problem to offering solutions to it.

Effortless phrases like 'just think' and 'just one' imply that the solutions suggested are realistic and achievable.

⑩ Practice

Write three paragraphs in response to this exam-style question.

'Young people have enough to think about without working as well. People under the age of 18 should not have jobs.'
Write a letter to a broadsheet newspaper in which you explain your point of view on this statement.

 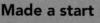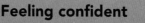

Rhetorical techniques

Use a variety of rhetorical techniques to engage the reader and add emphasis to important ideas.

 Examples of rhetorical techniques

Direct address and rhetorical questions

Direct address is an effective way to engage your reader. It involves the reader in your ideas and helps them understand your viewpoint. It can be used to build a conversational, understanding tone: *You try to resist, but that takeaway pizza is just too tempting.*

In a rhetorical question, direct address guides the reader to think about their own point of view: *How do you deal with exam stress?*

It can also prompt the reader to relate to a person or situation: *How would you feel?*

Emotive language

Choose emotive language to guide the reader's response. For example, positive, exciting words will motivate them to take action: *Volunteering is a brilliant way to make new friends and get involved in your local community.*

Sympathetic language will make the reader feel guilt or concern: *Tiny puppies as young as three weeks old are abandoned in the streets.*

> Think carefully about your form, audience and purpose when choosing rhetorical techniques. For example, hyperbole would be effective in a humorous tabloid article, but would not be suitable for a serious essay.

Repetition, lists and patterns of three

Repetition is particularly effective in speeches. It can be used to emphasise or exaggerate a key point: *We are doing too little, too late.*

A list works in a similar way to draw attention to a point and make it more compelling: *Cycling keeps you fit, boosts your immune system, saves you money and makes you feel great!* This list shows the writer's enthusiasm by highlighting how many benefits there are to cycling.

Repeating or listing things in patterns of three has a particularly satisfying effect, making an idea sound persuasive: *Walking, cycling and public transport are all green alternatives to driving.*

Hyperbole

Hyperbole can be used in speeches or less formal writing to humorously exaggerate a point. This entertains the reader and helps them to relate to an emotion or idea: *Exams are inhumane. Students are forced to revise night and day, barely sleeping and going grey in the process.* In this example, hyperbole helps the reader to sympathise with how stressful students find exams.

> When writing non-fiction, you can also use the figurative language techniques on page 9 and rhetorical devices on page 37.

 Worked example

'The internet has transformed the way we work, rest and play. It has changed our lives for the better.'

Write an article for a broadsheet newspaper in which you explain your point of view on this statement. **[40 marks]**

Can you imagine life without your phone, tablet or computer?

Critics argue that living our lives online is harming our social skills and attention spans, but the internet has many benefits. It makes us faster, friendlier and more effective.

Being better connected has a huge impact on our social and family lives. One study found that 53% of participants felt their family was more connected now they use the internet. Social media and messaging services make it easy to share our lives with our loved ones without the awkward silences or extortionate phone bills.

The internet is not just about talking to your grandmother and your friends, though. It puts a whole world of information at our fingertips. Whether finding out about current affairs, researching homework, or revising for exams, the internet keeps us better informed...

| Rhetorical questions engage the reader. | Lists can be used to persuasive effect. This pattern of three shows that there are many ways in which the internet keeps people informed. | Emotive language provokes a response. |

 Practice

Write three paragraphs of your response to this exam-style question, including at least one rhetorical device in each.

> 'Charities are a lifeline for vulnerable people. We should all give more to support them.'
> Write an article for a broadsheet newspaper in which you explain your point of view on this statement.

Using tone, style and register

You should tailor your tone, style and register to suit your form, audience and purpose. This will help you to have the strongest effect on the reader.

② Tone, style and register

In Paper 2, Question 5 you will need to write in a largely formal register, using Standard English. However, for some audiences you may wish to include some occasional informal language.

Choose your language carefully to create an effective tone and style. By producing a particular atmosphere you can guide the reader to respond in a particular way.

For example, using emotive language and the strong verb 'must' creates a serious, urgent tone to inspire the reader to take action: Our precious planet is dying. We must do something before it is too late.

Go to page 38 to revise tone, style and register.

⑤ Worked example

'People worry too much about the dangers of fast food. There is nothing wrong with a treat now and then.'

Write a letter to your headteacher in which you explain your viewpoint about this statement.

[40 marks]

Dear Ms Robson,

I am writing to raise my concerns about fast food being served in the school canteen. I appreciate that everyone needs an occasional treat, but offering burgers, pizza and chips every day is too much of a temptation for many...

⑤ Worked example

'People worry too much about the dangers of fast food. There is nothing wrong with a treat now and then.'

Write an article for your school or college newspaper in which you explain your point of view on this statement. **[40 marks]**

Healthy eating is a good thing. But not all the time.

Studying for your GCSEs is a really stressful time, without the added guilt about that bacon sarnie you had for breakfast. Students need to give themselves a break now and then and enjoy a well-earned trashy treat...

Use colloquial language such as 'trashy treat' to create a relaxed style.

Address the reader directly using 'you' to create a conversational tone.

② Form, audience and purpose

The tone, style and register of your writing need to suit the form, audience and purpose you have been given.

For example, an entertaining article in your school or college newspaper might have a light-hearted tone, conversational style and formal register with a few less formal words to engage the audience. In contrast, a letter to your local MP should have a serious tone, persuasive style and formal register.

For the most effective approach, you may wish to add a little variety. A sudden change in tone could have a dramatic effect in a newspaper article, for example.

A serious tone, a mature style and a formal register are most appropriate for writing a letter to an adult.

Use fewer contractions in a formal register.

Consider the difference between 'fast food being served in the school canteen' (passive voice emphasises 'fast food') and 'the school canteen serving fast food' (active voice emphasises the 'school canteen').

Choose sophisticated, precise vocabulary to create a mature style.

Add a counterargument to deal with opposing views and demonstrate that you are taking the issue seriously.

This task asks you to write an article for an audience of young people. An entertaining tone, a conversational style and an informal register would be most effective.

Use short, punchy sentences to suggest a less formal register.

⑩ Practice

Write the opening two paragraphs of your response to this exam-style question, thinking carefully about tone, style and register.

'Pets are a big responsibility. Only people over the age of 18 should be allowed to own one.'

Write an article for a broadsheet newspaper in which you explain your point of view on this statement.

Articles

In Paper 2, Question 5 you might be asked to write an article. This is a piece of writing about a particular topic, usually written for a magazine, newspaper or website.

(2) Structural features

Your article should include:
- ☑ appropriate headings for the type of article you are writing – in the exam, write these in your normal handwriting
- ☑ an engaging opening that outlines your main point of view
- ☑ short, clear paragraphs
- ☑ evidence such as quotations from experts or eyewitnesses
- ☑ a conclusion that reiterates your main point of view in a memorable way.

(2) Headings

Use headings to make your article more authentic.

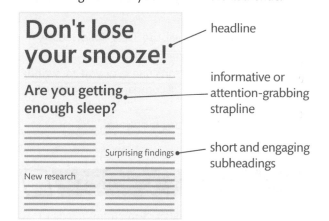

Don't lose your snooze! — headline

Are you getting enough sleep? — informative or attention-grabbing strapline

New research / Surprising findings — short and engaging subheadings

(10) Worked example

'Teenagers these days are increasingly badly behaved. We are raising a generation of thugs and criminals.'

Write an article for a broadsheet newspaper in which you give your point of view on this statement.

[40 marks]

The truth about teenagers ◄

As another negative report about teenagers is published, is it time to ask whether teenagers are all as bad as we are led to believe? ◄

If you believe most media reports, it seems the streets are full of violent, threatening youths behaving like animals and terrorising the elderly.

There are, of course, a minority of teenagers who regularly commit crimes and vandalise their neighbourhoods. But how often do we remember that most young people are well-behaved and hard-working members of our society? A new report published today does just that... ◄

So, next time you read a hysterical story about the youth of today, remember the 32% who regularly volunteer for charities, the thousands who already run their own businesses, and the 84% who want to make the world a better place. ◄

End with a strong conclusion to leave a lasting impression on the reader. Here, a call to action with a list of three striking statistics guides the reader to reconsider their own opinion.

(2) Tabloid or broadsheet?

Tabloid newspapers focus on entertainment. Their stories are often more light-hearted, which is reflected in shorter sentences, a dramatic or humorous tone and less formal language.

Broadsheet newspapers are more serious and detailed. They generally use longer, more complex sentences and formal language, but informal language might be used sparingly to lighten the tone.

Use a short, simple headline to grab the reader's attention and suggest what the article is about. Here, alliteration makes the headline more striking.

Begin by introducing your point of view in an engaging strapline of one or two sentences. Here, a rhetorical question makes the reader consider their own opinion.

Break down your main points into short, clear paragraphs. Here, a new paragraph is used to show a change in perspective.

Use statistics and expert evidence to support your points and make your ideas sound believable and trustworthy.

(10) Practice

Write a headline, subheading and opening paragraph for a tabloid newspaper article in which you agree with the statement in the exam-style question above.

Letters

If you are asked to write a letter in Paper 2, Question 5, make sure you include an appropriate greeting and sign-off.

Greetings

A letter should always begin with an appropriate greeting.

- If you know the person well, use 'Dear' and their first name: *Dear Katy*
- If you don't know them well, use 'Dear' followed by their title and surname: *Dear Mr Lees*
- If you don't know the person's name, or you are writing to an organisation such as a company or newspaper, use *Dear Sir/Madam*
- A comma after your greeting is optional.

 Signing off

Your sign-off depends on which greeting you have used.

- If you greeted the person by name, end with 'Yours sincerely' and your name. If you don't know them personally, give your first name and surname.
- If you began with 'Dear Sir/Madam', end with 'Yours faithfully' followed by your first name and surname.
- Remember that 'Yours' is always capitalised, whereas 'sincerely' and 'faithfully' are not.
- A comma after 'Yours sincerely' or 'Yours faithfully' is optional.

Worked example

'We are a nation of litterbugs. Something needs to be done about the state of our cities.'

Write a letter to your local council in which you explain your point of view on this statement.

[40 marks]

Dear Sir/Madam,

Our city has some of the finest parks in the country. For instance, Treetops Park has won many awards in the last ten years. However, I am writing to express my concern at the unacceptable amount of litter that is spoiling our city's green spaces.

First and foremost, litter is a danger to the health and safety of people who want to enjoy our parks. Yesterday I took my younger sister to the children's play area in Treetops Park only to find it littered with broken glass...

I hope that you will take action now to make our parks clean and safe for everyone to enjoy.

Yours faithfully,

Ashish Akram

If you don't know the reader personally, sign off with your first name and surname.

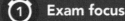 Exam focus

In your exam, you do not need to include a postal address in your letter. Show that you are using the correct form by using a greeting and a sign-off.

Use the correct greeting. Here, 'Dear Sir/Madam' is used because a name isn't given in the question.

In the first paragraph, gain the reader's attention and explain why you are writing.

Choose your tone and register carefully. A letter to an adult you don't know personally will require formal vocabulary. In this example, 'unacceptable' formally expresses a negative opinion without sounding rude.

The middle section should develop your ideas in clearly structured paragraphs. Start a new paragraph for each of your key points.

End your letter with a polite request for the reader to take action.

The sign-off should reflect your greeting. 'Yours faithfully' is used here because the letter began 'Dear Sir/Madam'.

Practice

Write the greeting, first paragraph, last paragraph and sign-off of your response to this exam-style question.

'The school day is too short. Students should be working longer hours to prepare them for their adult working lives.'

Write a letter to your headteacher in which you explain your point of view on this statement.

Speeches

In Paper 2, Question 5, you may be asked to write a speech. In a speech, you need to tailor your language and structure to hold your audience's attention.

② Language

A speech has a listening audience rather than a reading one, and you need to tailor your language to reflect this. Avoid very long, complex sentences so that your audience can easily follow your ideas. Choose engaging language that creates a dramatic and emotive style to keep the audience's attention. You could use:

- rhetorical questions
- direct address
- emotive and figurative language.

Go to page 67 to revise rhetorical techniques.

② Structure

The structure of a speech needs to guide the audience through your argument. You should include:

- an effective opening
- logically organised ideas
- a strong conclusion
- adverbials to help the reader follow the direction of your ideas
- features, such as facts, anecdotes and expert opinion, to support your ideas.

Go to page 65 to revise directing the reader and page 75 to revise structuring non-fiction.

⑩ Worked example

'There is too much litter on our streets. We should all take more responsibility for our environment.'

Write a speech to deliver at your local community centre in which you explain your point of view on this statement.

[40 marks]

Is there a carpet of litter in your park? Unfortunately, litter is now part of our lives in Britain. In fact, a recent survey suggested that it is so common that many of us no longer even notice it.

I am here today to talk to you about the many problems that litter creates. It doesn't just spoil our streets and parks. It costs our councils millions of pounds a year to clean it up. Tragically, this is money that could be spent on our hospitals, schools and care homes, which are already struggling for cash.

Significantly, over 60% of the litter on our streets and in our parks is abandoned soft-drink cans and food containers. It is time we forced shops and fast-food companies to take action...

So, don't just sit there. Let's all take action. Let's get out and do something before our country becomes one big, rotting rubbish bin.

Grab your audience's attention in your first paragraph. In this example, a rhetorical question makes them think of their own local park.

Use direct address to build a relationship with the audience. This is a key feature of a speech. Inclusive pronouns such as 'we' and 'us' can also be used to create this effect.

Use paragraphs to structure your ideas clearly. Keep your paragraphs fairly short and start a new paragraph for each key idea.

Choose emotive language to encourage an emotional reaction. 'Tragically' might make the audience feel upset or guilty about the loss of money to help vulnerable people.

Use adverbials to guide your audience through your ideas. Here, 'significantly' highlights an important piece of information.

Use facts and statistics to support your ideas and sound knowledgeable to the audience.

End with a strong conclusion. Speeches often end with a warning or a rousing call for action to prompt the reader to get involved.

⑩ Practice

Write the opening and ending of your response to this exam-style question.

'A uniform brings a school together. It is important that uniform rules are respected.'

Write a speech to present at your school or college in which you explain your point of view on this statement.

Essays

You may be asked to write an essay in Paper 2, Question 5. This is a formal piece of writing directed at an audience with knowledge of the subject matter.

Register

Essays are serious pieces of writing for an audience who are interested in the topic, so the register must be formal. Your tone should be professional and knowledgeable. Even though you are expressing a point of view, you should try to make your points using a style that is objective and impersonal.

To achieve this you could:

- use sophisticated vocabulary choices
- avoid contractions
- use expert opinions to back up your points
- use facts and statistics to make your points sound trustworthy.

Structure

First paragraph

Briefly introduce your opinion.

Main body

Develop and defend your opinion. Use a new paragraph for each new idea and make links between them using adverbial phrases to build up a convincing picture of your point of view.

Conclusion

Summarise what you have said in a memorable way.

Worked example

'Healthy eating is the key to living a long and happy life. We must educate young people so that they make healthier food choices.'

Write an essay for a fitness journal in which you explain your point of view on this statement.

[40 marks]

Today's world is flooded with social media posts, TV adverts and billboards advertising unhealthy food. Tempting images of attractive cupcakes and towering burgers surround us constantly. Today more than ever, young people need to be educated so that they can make healthier choices, live longer and be happier.

Firstly, parents are not doing enough to educate young people about the dangers of unhealthy eating. While around half of primary school children are given a packed lunch to take to school, over 50% of these lunches contain too many unhealthy snacks according to government guidelines...

In conclusion, schools, parents and the media are all failing young people. Health is the key to a long and happy life, and it is our duty to give young people the necessary knowledge to help them make the right choices.

Engage the reader with rhetorical features, but keep the overall tone formal. Here, a list is used to highlight the number of temptations.

Clearly outline your opinion in the first paragraph.

Use the passive voice to create a sophisticated, formal tone.

Start a new paragraph for each point, and begin each paragraph with a topic sentence outlining its main point.

Use statistics to support your ideas and make your writing sound authoritative.

End with a conclusion to sum up your main ideas and emphasise your opinion, being careful not to repeat yourself. If the essay is strongly argumentative then a call to action might be appropriate.

Use sophisticated vocabulary to create a professional tone. Here 'it is our duty' is used instead of 'we must'.

Practice

Write the first three paragraphs and the final paragraph of your response to this exam-style question.

'Young people need to know how to keep themselves safe. Self-defence should be taught in schools.'

Write an essay for a parenting journal in which you explain your point of view on this statement.

  Made a start **Feeling confident** 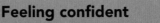 **Exam ready**

Leaflets

In Paper 2, Question 5, you may be asked to write a leaflet. Leaflets provide information and advice in a clear, structured way.

② Key features

A leaflet should convey information and ideas in a clear way. Use these key features to break information into manageable sections for the reader:

- a title
- subheadings
- bullet points
- numbered lists.

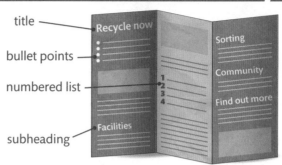

title

bullet points

numbered list

subheading

⑩ Worked example

'Exam stress affects the wellbeing of many young people and they need to know how to cope.'

Write a leaflet for GCSE students in which you explain your point of view on this statement.

[40 marks]

<u>Coping with exam stress</u>

The word 'exam' is enough to fill the heart of every Year 11 student with terror. A few nerves to kick-start your revision might be useful, but if you are losing sleep or not feeling your usual self, it is time to take action.

Exam stress can affect anyone, no matter how smart, laid-back or well-prepared they are. That's why it's so important to know the signs and understand how to deal with them.

<u>Common signs of stress</u>

Although different people show stress in different ways, look out for some of these common signs of stress:

- trouble concentrating
- low energy levels
- low mood
- inability to sleep
- constant worrying.

...If you are worried that you, or a friend, are suffering from exam stress, follow these three steps:

1. Talk to someone.
2. Make a revision timetable.
3. Eat well and exercise regularly.

Use numbered lists to highlight important points or clearly show the steps the reader must follow.

① Exam focus

Bullet points and numbered lists are useful features of the leaflet form. However, use them sparingly and make sure that most of your writing is in paragraphed prose to show off your writing skills.

Clearly explain the leaflet's purpose in the title.

Engage the reader with careful language choices. Here, figurative language appeals to the reader's senses to remind them of how it feels to be nervous.

Develop your writing by using subheadings to guide the reader through your ideas.

Consider your audience. In this example, the language is formal, but not overly so. This relaxed tone would appeal to an audience of young people.

Use bullet points to present information in a clear way. Make sure each bullet point is short and simple.

End your leaflet with useful advice or a call to action to make an impact on the reader.

⑩ Practice

Write the first three paragraphs of your response to this exam-style question.

'Families spend too much time slumped in front of the TV together.' Write a leaflet for parents in which you explain how they can make the most of the free time they have with their children.

Gathering non-fiction ideas

Considering arguments for and against a statement is a good way to start planning your answer for Paper 2, Question 5.

(2) Getting started ☑

Plan your time carefully. You should spend:
- 5 minutes planning
- 35 minutes writing
- 5 minutes checking your work.

Read the question carefully and underline the key words. Before you start writing, you need to be sure of:
- the audience
- the purpose
- the form
- the topic.

(2) Planning ☑

1. In a table, quickly write down as many ideas as you can for and against the statement in the question.

2. Then, decide on which point of view to take. You could use your own personal opinion or whichever side has the most persuasive arguments to help you craft an effective response to the task.

3. Read your points again, crossing out the weaker ones.

4. Number your most effective points to show the order in which you will use them. You could use some of the opposing points you came up with as counterarguments.

(5) Worked example ☑

'Too many <u>young people</u> are <u>wasting</u> their <u>time</u> and <u>money</u> on <u>gap years</u>. Their time would be better spent as an apprentice learning a trade.'

Write an <u>article for a broadsheet newspaper</u> in which you <u>explain your point of view</u> on this statement.

Underline the key words in the question. **[40 marks]**

Plan

For – young people should get into work	Against – gap years are valuable
• Work experience is useful	• Teach independence (1)
• Gap years are expensive	• Experience different cultures – good for society (3)
• Might get into trouble on gap year	• Helps you figure out what you want to do in life (5)
• Travellers are ruining important historical sites – counterargument against point 3?	• ~~See the world~~
	• Voluntary work (4)
	• Saving up is good experience in budgeting (2)
	• ~~Last chance to spend time with childhood friends~~
	• ~~Good fun~~

Start thinking about how you will link your ideas.

Cross out arguments that are less likely to appeal to the audience, or that don't answer the question directly.

(10) Practice ☑

Make a table of arguments for and against the statement in this exam-style question.

'The internet brings out the worst in people. All social media should be banned in schools.'

Write a speech to be given to students in your school or college in which you explain your point of view on this statement.

☑ **Made a start** ☑ **Feeling confident** ☑ **Exam ready**

Structuring non-fiction

Structure your non-fiction writing carefully to guide the reader through your argument and emphasise your key ideas.

 Clarity and impact

Use structure to give your writing both clarity and impact. You can do this by:

- starting with an attention-grabbing idea to engage the reader from the start
- saving your most shocking or memorable idea until the end to leave the reader with a lasting impression
- starting with simpler ideas to ease the reader in, then building up to more complex ideas
- making links between your points to make them easy to follow and demonstrate how they build up to a convincing whole.

 Worked example

'Young people are responsible for most of the serious accidents on the roads today. For safety, the minimum age for driving should be raised to 25.'

Write a letter to your local MP in which you explain your point of view on this statement.

Plan   **[40 marks]**

Dear Ms Khan...

Introduction: young people need to drive

1. Only a minority are careless (use expert opinion)

2. Make tracker boxes compulsory to limit speed

3. Old people are just as dangerous.
   - Drive too slowly, cause road rage (use anecdote)
   - Slower reactions

4. Many young people need to drive for their job
   - Would restrict career choices, give examples of jobs needing car (example: cousin is a charity worker)

5. Counterargument
   Some people think not mature enough at 17
   But mature enough to join army and fight?

6. Public transport not good enough
   - Government needs to take action to improve if driving age raised (use statistics to show that local buses are unreliable and expensive)

Conclusion: Call to action – vote against this idea, young people are your supporters of the future!

Yours sincerely...

Include an appropriate opening in your plan.
Start with a simple idea to ease the reader in.
Consider offering an alternative solution to make your point of view seem more balanced and reasonable.
Add an anecdote to add human interest. You can make this up if you like.
Slowly build up to your most complicated and hard-hitting ideas. This shows your argument developing and will help the reader to follow it.
Use evidence such as statistics to support your opinions.
Use direct address to end with a strong conclusion.
Include an appropriate ending. A letter should end with a sign-off, whereas a speech might end with a final address to the audience.

 Practice

Write a plan for this exam-style question.

'The internet generation has become disconnected from reality and is incapable of dealing with the real world. It is time to introduce a legal age limit for owning a smartphone.'

Write a letter to your local MP in which you explain your point of view on this statement.

Paper 2, Question 5

Paper 2, Question 5 will be a non-fiction writing task. Look at this worked example and then try the exam-style practice.

 Worked example

'Donating money to charity is a waste of time. Charities constantly pester us for money but they never make any real difference to people's lives.'

Write a speech to be given at your local community centre in which you explain your point of view on this statement.

(24 marks for content and organisation

16 marks for technical accuracy)

[40 marks]

Last weekend I ran 26 miles. My first marathon was thrilling, but not something I am going to repeat in a hurry. However, as I ran for the finish line, my thoughts were not on my aching feet, my gasping breath or my cramped legs. They were on the hundreds of pounds I was raising for Cancer Relief.

Donating to charity is difficult to avoid these days. We are constantly pestered with requests for our hard-earned cash. In fact, a recent report suggests that we receive over ten requests every day for our money.

Therefore, it is no surprise that many people have switched off from charity. They feel that charities bully people for money. For example, there are many reports of older people being pressured into giving. Smiling young people turn up on their doorsteps waving pictures of starving puppies or cute kittens and refuse to leave until they have got a donation.

However, there is no doubt that many small charities would struggle to survive without our help. In my home town, a charity raises money each year to run a holiday club for young people with disabilities. Nobody there is paid, but they work really hard to raise money that helps to change young people's lives...

It is easy to ignore all those charities fighting for our attention, or to think that our money won't make a difference. But every pound counts, and everyone has a pound to spare. So choose a charity that is close to your heart and sign up online in the comfort of your own home. Or alternatively, get your trainers on, get outside and get fit while you're giving!

Finish with a memorable ending. Choose the technique that will be most effective for your audience and form. A call to action works well in this speech.

The form of this task is a speech, which requires engaging and emotive language. The audience is likely to be mixed, so a formal but relaxed tone is most appropriate.

Check your writing to make sure your spelling, punctuation and grammar are accurate.

Make your opening as engaging as possible. Here, an anecdote is used to build a relationship with the audience.

Use language features such as a pattern of three to emphasise a point. Here, it highlights the writer's struggle in the marathon, making it sound even more impressive.

Use a counterargument to demonstrate that your opinion is reasonable and well thought out. However, make sure you keep the focus on your own opinion. This example begins with a counterargument, which is then dismissed by a change in perspective.

Use 'we' to create an inclusive, friendly tone and imply an understanding with the audience.

Use adverbials to signpost key evidence and guide the audience through your ideas.

Choose emotive language to help the audience to share your feelings.

Think carefully about tone and register. In this example, colloquial language is used to create a light and friendly tone that would appeal to a mixed audience. This makes the serious topic more engaging and accessible.

Give evidence such as facts, statistics or expert opinions to support your ideas. Here, the writer has used an anecdote for a more personal approach.

 Exam-style practice

'Reality TV is full of ageing has-beens and talentless people desperate to be famous. Watching it is a waste of time.'

Write a speech to be given at your school or college in which you explain your point of view on this statement.

[40 marks]

  Made a start **Feeling confident** **Exam ready**

Beginning a sentence

A sentence should always begin with a capital letter. Vary your sentence openings to create deliberate effects and emphasise important information.

 Sentence openings

The beginning of a sentence sets the tone for what follows. Different word types will shape the reader's response in different ways. Go to page 5 to revise word classes.

A pronoun

In fiction, beginning with a pronoun will focus the reader's attention on a particular character: He charged into the classroom just in time.

In non-fiction, a first-person pronoun can be used to highlight your own opinion: I believe that a lack of sunshine has a serious effect on mood.

A verb

Beginning with a verb emphasises a movement or action. This is particularly effective in fiction writing: Edging silently forwards, I strained to hear the whispers from behind the door.

An adverb

In fiction, starting a sentence with an adverb gives the reader a detailed image of how a character is performing an action: Slowly, I reached out and grabbed his hand.

In non-fiction, adverbials signal where your argument will go next, making it easier for the reader to follow: In contrast, many parents are in favour of extra homework.

A conjunction

In both fiction and non-fiction, starting a sentence with a conjunction allows you to position the most significant idea at the end of the sentence, giving it added emphasis.

While studying abroad isn't for everyone, it can be a life-changing experience for many.

When I think back to that day, I can't help but shudder.

An adjective

Starting a sentence with an adjective is a good way to make a description more effective in both fiction and non-fiction: Violent criminals are being treated like royalty in our prisons.

A preposition

A preposition highlights the relationship between one thing and another. In fiction, this can help the reader to picture the layout of a scene: Behind me, I could hear Hana and Nikki sniggering.

In non-fiction, prepositions draw attention to the connection between ideas or things: Despite our efforts, global warming is still increasing.

 Variation for effect

Experiment with rearranging your sentences to create different effects:

I crouched down slowly, and peered through the branches.	Starting with a pronoun draws attention to the narrator and the danger they are in.
Crouching slowly, I peered through the branches.	Starting with a verb draws attention to the narrator's crouching action, suggesting their fear.
Slowly, I crouched down and peered through the branches.	Starting with an adverb emphasises how carefully the narrator is trying not to draw attention to themselves.

 Exam focus

Don't force different sentence structures into your writing just for the sake of variety. Always choose the approach that will most successfully create the effect you want to have on the reader.

 Practice

Write two paragraphs in response to this exam-style question, focusing on choosing the most effective sentence beginnings.

> You are going to enter a creative writing competition at your school or college.
>
> Your entry will be judged by a panel of teachers.
>
> Write the opening part of a story about an exotic place.

Ending a sentence

Make sure the punctuation at the end of your sentences is accurate and effective.

⑤ Full stops

Full stops should be used at the end of any sentence that isn't a question or an exclamation.

The most common mistake to make with full stops is the **comma splice**. This is where a comma is used to join two sentences when a full stop should have been used to separate them instead:

Animal testing is wrong, it is a cruel way to treat other creatures.

These two pieces of information are independent and should therefore be separated by a full stop:

Animal testing is wrong. It is a cruel way to treat other creatures.

Alternatively, they could be joined with a conjunction:

Animal testing is wrong because it is a cruel way to treat other creatures.

① Aiming higher ⬆

In some cases, a semi-colon can be used to correct a comma splice without adding a conjunction:

Animal testing is wrong; it is a cruel way to treat other creatures.

This strongly connects the two clauses.

Go to page 79 to revise semi-colons.

② Ellipses

In fiction, ellipses can be used to make dialogue sound authentic:

'Surely you haven't…'
Here, an ellipsis suggests the speaker has trailed off, as if they cannot bear to go on.

'It isn't… I mean… I haven't…'
In this example, ellipses suggest that the speaker is struggling to find the right words to express themselves. It might imply fear or nervousness.

② Question marks

All questions, including rhetorical ones, should end in a question mark:

Was your mascara tested on this innocent puppy?

A sentence usually needs a question mark if:

- it begins with a question word such as 'why' or 'what'
- your voice rises at the end when you read it aloud.

Make sure you don't use a question mark for indirect (or reported) speech:

Her friend asked her whether she thought testing make-up on animals was wrong.

② Exclamation marks

Used correctly, exclamation marks can add drama or humour to fiction and non-fiction writing. Make sure you follow these rules:

- Only use an exclamation mark for a real exclamation: *'I can't believe it!' she cried.*
- Never use two or more exclamation marks in a row.
- Use exclamation marks sparingly – overuse reduces their impact.

You can also use ellipses to show where words have been left out of quoted text. Go to page 13 to revise how to quote texts concisely.

② Aiming higher ⬆

Avoid using ellipses to suggest tension or create a cliffhanger at the end of a story, as this can be predictable. Try to create tension through language choice and sentence structure instead.

⑩ Practice

Rewrite this paragraph, correcting the comma splices with appropriate punctuation.

You often hear that a dog is for life, but do the vast majority of people who repeat this cliché fully appreciate what it implies, no, puppies are small and cuddly, too many new dog owners fail to realise they will soon grow, after a year or more they are puppies no longer, they have grown into huge dogs needing vast amounts of exercise, vast amounts of food and vast amounts of attention. All too often, the result is disaster, it's not just furniture that gets chewed and destroyed, people can be hurt by dogs that have become aggressive through lack of training or lack of care. Will we as a society continue to permit this, it remains to be seen.

✓ **Made a start** ✓ **Feeling confident** ✓ **Exam ready**

Commas, semi-colons & colons

Commas, semi-colons and colons break up sentences. Use them to develop the complexity of your ideas and express yourself clearly.

② Commas in lists

Commas are used to separate the items in a list. In most cases, you should use a comma after each item except the final two:

I love walking in the countryside. It doesn't matter if it is cold, rainy, windy, sunny or snowing!

Sometimes, a comma is used after the second-to-last item in a list to make the meaning clearer:

She ordered soup, fish and chips, and ice cream.

Here, the extra comma shows that the ice cream is separate from the fish and chips.

② Aiming higher ⬆

It is vital to punctuate your writing accurately. It helps you to express your ideas clearly and precisely. Using a wider range of more sophisticated punctuation, such as colons, semi-colons and dashes, can help you to express your ideas with even greater precision – but only if they are used correctly.

⑤ Colons

1 Colons can be used to introduce a phrase or main clause containing extra information:

My brother is only nice to me twice a year: on my birthday and at Christmas.

phrase with extra information

Cycling is my passion: I just love being outside in the fresh air.

main clause with extra information

2 They can also be used to introduce lists:

Cycling can improve your life in so many ways: your health, your mood, your finances and your looks all benefit.

3 You can also use them to introduce quotations:

Professor Kaur is keen to share her findings: 'This is vital information for every parent.'

⑤ Commas and clauses

Commas are also used to separate the clauses in some multi-clause sentences.

1 If a subordinate clause comes before the main clause, you should use a comma to separate them:

subordinate clause ~~~~ main clause

Whenever I see people sitting in traffic, I walk faster and smile.

If the main clause comes first, you don't need a comma:

main clause ~~~~ subordinate clause

I walk faster and smile whenever I see people sitting in traffic.

2 Use commas and 'which' for a relative clause that isn't essential to the meaning of a sentence:

The post office, which had been shut the previous day, was very crowded.
non-essential relative clause

Use 'that' and no commas for a relative clause that is essential to the meaning of a sentence:

The cookies that have chocolate chips in them are my favourites.
essential relative clause

⑤ Semi-colons

1 Use semi-colons to separate a list of detailed items that contain commas:

The study was conducted by Dr Siobhan O'Keefe, lecturer in Psychology at the University of Newton; Professor Sana Kaur, researcher in Developmental Psychology at the University of Ashington; and child behaviour expert Dr Mike Pickles.

Use a semi-colon before 'and', too.

2 You can also use semi-colons to show a close connection between two main clauses:

Cycling is good for you; it gets you outdoors.

In fiction, this can be used to build tension.

I couldn't breathe; I was speechless with fear.

⑩ Practice

Write two paragraphs in response to this exam-style question, using all of the punctuation marks described on this page.

> 'Cars are one of the biggest factors in global warming. If we are to save the planet, we must improve public transport and make cycling and walking safer in our cities.'
>
> Write a letter to your local MP in which you explain your point of view on this statement.

Other punctuation

Make sure you use apostrophes, speech marks and inverted commas accurately to express your ideas clearly.

Apostrophes in contractions

A contraction is where two words have been joined together with some letters missed out to make them shorter. An apostrophe shows where letters have been removed:

Elderly people shouldn't have to spend Christmas alone.

Here, the 'should' and 'not' have been combined. The apostrophe shows that the 'o' from 'not' is missing.

Contractions make your writing more informal. In Paper 2, Question 5 always think carefully about whether they are appropriate for your audience, purpose and form.

Speech marks

You should always use speech marks in direct speech, such as dialogue in fiction writing. Follow these rules:

- Enclose the spoken words and punctuation in speech marks:

  'Stay right there.'

- You should usually begin speech with a capital letter, and always end it with a punctuation mark, such as a comma, a full stop, a question mark or an exclamation mark:

  'Why should I?' I whispered.

- To state who is speaking, end the speech with a comma and continue without a capital letter (unless the next word is a proper noun):

  'I'm glad that's over,' sighed Mum.

- If you state who is speaking at the start of the sentence, introduce the speech with a comma:

  He turned and shouted, 'Stop!'

- You don't need a capital letter if you are continuing a sentence of speech:

  'I didn't mean to drop it,' Tara said, blushing, 'it just slipped out of my hand.'

- Start a new paragraph and a new set of speech marks each time the speaker changes:

  'I can't believe it!' grinned James.
  'This is the best day ever!' cheered Ibrahim.

Apostrophes and possession

An apostrophe is attached to a noun to show that it is the owner of something. The apostrophe should always be attached to the owner, not the object.

With a **singular noun** (just one person or thing), add an apostrophe and an 's':

My brother's dog ran off.

Mr Jones's first name is Joseph.

Follow the same rule for a **plural noun** (a group of people or things) that does not end in an 's':

Our children's education is at risk.

However, if the plural ends in an 's', you should add an apostrophe but not an 's':

The cyclists' helmets gleamed.

Quotation marks

Speech marks are also used as quotation marks.

1. Use quotation marks at the beginning and end of titles:

   'Macbeth' is a play of murder and magic.

2. In the reading section of your exam, use quotation marks when you repeat the exact words from a source. Go to page 13 to revise this.

3. In non-fiction writing, use quotation marks when you repeat someone's exact words, such as when giving expert evidence:

   Lisa Davies explains, 'A warm-up routine is vital, even before a short run.'

Indirect speech

Indirect speech does not need speech marks:

Quinn said that he was going to the park.

Here, Quinn's words have been reported, so they do not need speech marks.

Exam focus

You can use either single or double speech marks for direct speech and quotations, but make sure you are consistent.

Practice

Rewrite this paragraph, correcting the errors.

In his blog How to Stay Healthy, Obasi Okeke states that even a small amount of exercise can make a big difference. It doesnt matter how long you spend exercising. What matters is that you do something regularly' He explains. Okekes view is that we can all spare 20 minute's each morning. His motto is: 'theres nothing more important than your health'.

  Made a start **Feeling confident** **Exam ready**

Parentheses

A parenthesis is a piece of non-essential information in a sentence, usually separated from the rest of the sentence by dashes or brackets.

Brackets

Brackets can be used to add extra information to a sentence as a phrase or clause. They should always be used in pairs, and can come in the middle or at the end of the sentence. The sentence's closing punctuation should always come outside the brackets:

Parents (even those who never got told off at school) were young and impulsive once.

Many people doubted that I would be brave enough to stand up to him (including my own mother).

You can also use brackets to add a whole sentence of extra information. In this case, the sentence's closing punctuation should be placed inside the brackets.

My local football team has been struggling for as long as I can remember. (The last time they won a title was in 1999.)

Dashes

Dashes are another way to add extra information. They are often used to explain or expand on the main part of the sentence.

Use a pair of dashes to add information in the middle of a sentence:

Several years ago – although it still feels like yesterday – I decided to take a stand.

Use a single dash to add information at the end of a sentence to suggest a pause or afterthought:

Sometimes I forget how many risks I took as a child – then I remember the swimming pool incident.

Adding information as an afterthought is an effective way to make your dialogue or narrative voice sound authentic:

I made the decision to go – although maybe I shouldn't have agreed so quickly.

This extra information reveals the narrator's doubt, suggesting that they are indecisive.

Parentheses in fiction

Use parentheses in fiction to develop a character's speech or add personality to the narrative voice.

Asides

An aside has a similar effect to a comment you would say under your breath. It can be used to create humour and build a feeling of closeness with the reader:

I saw Aunt Marie at the shops again. (She's always spending money!)

In this aside, the narrator shares a judgement about Aunt Marie's shopping habits. This implies that they disapprove.

Tangents

A tangent is where a character or narrator goes off topic:

My cousins live in Australia (the driest inhabited continent on earth).

This tangent suggests that the narrator is enthusiastic about geography facts.

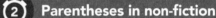 Parentheses in non-fiction

Use parentheses in non-fiction texts to give the reader additional information:

Dr Xiu (who has successfully treated sports injuries for many world-class athletes) is a firm believer in the power of positive thinking.

The information in this parenthesis suggests that the reader should take this expert's opinion seriously.

You can also use parentheses to create humour or lighten the tone of your writing:

Many of the world's most successful business people left school without any qualifications. (But don't tell your teenagers that, unless you want a battle when revision time comes around!)

Here, humour lightens the tone and builds a friendly relationship with the reader.

Exam focus

Although marks are awarded for using a range of punctuation, make sure you are using it to good effect and not overdoing it. Think about how the techniques shown on this page can add to the impact of your writing.

Practice

Write a paragraph in response to this exam-style question, using brackets and dashes in your answer.

'Where you choose to go on holiday is not important. It's the people you go with that make a holiday great.'

Write an article for a broadsheet newspaper in which you explain your point of view on this statement.

Homophones

Homophones are words that sound the same but have different spellings and meanings. Learning common homophones will help you to avoid spelling mistakes.

(2) Their, there and they're

- 'Their' means 'belonging to them':
  Librarians love to share their ideas.

- 'There' is a place or position:
  The fiction section is over there.

- 'They're' is a contraction of 'they are':
  They're excited to be borrowing more books.

(2) Your and you're

- 'Your' means 'belonging to you':
  It's your decision.

- 'You're' is a contraction of 'you are':
  You're in control of the situation.

(2) Whose and who's

- 'Whose' expresses ownership or association:
  That famous author, whose latest book is out next month, visited our college recently.

- 'Who's' is a contraction of 'who is' or 'who has':
  I want to see who's playing before I buy tickets.

(2) Its and it's

- 'It's' is a contraction of 'it is':
  It's not surprising that young people have no interest in cooking.

- 'Its' means 'belonging to it':
  Our school is very proud of its modern facilities.

To decide which homophone to use, try replacing 'its' or 'it's' with 'it is'. If the sentence still makes sense, you should use the contraction 'it's':
It is important to take regular breaks from revision.

(2) To, two and too

- 'To' indicates place, direction or position:
  I first went to the local swimming pool when I was just a baby.

- 'Two' is a number:
  I'm lucky because my town has two parks.

- 'Too' means 'also' or 'an excessive amount':
  You can never have too many cafés.

(2) Our, are and hour

- 'Our' means 'belonging to us'.
- 'Are' is a form of the verb 'to be'.
- 'Hour' is a unit of time.
  Our teachers are all very keen to get young people reading for at least an hour a week.

(2) We're, wear, were and where

- 'We're' is a contraction of 'we are':
  We're all responsible for protecting our wildlife.

- 'Wear' is a verb meaning 'to be dressed in':
  I have to wear school uniform.

- 'Were' is the past tense of the verb 'are':
  The playing fields were shabby and unloved when I was young.

- 'Where' refers to place:
  Where is the train station?

This sentence makes sense with 'it is', so 'it's' would be correct. You can use this technique to check all the contractions on this page to see whether you are using them correctly.

(10) Practice

Choose the correct homophone to complete each of the sentences.

1. The description confuses the reader because they don't know we're/wear/were/where exactly the narrator is.

2. To/Two/Too many owners spend less than to/two/too hours a night with their/there/they're pets.

3. The lion shook its/it's mane and ran off into the trees.

4. When did you last consider your/you're effect on the environment?

Common spelling errors

Make sure you are aware of these common errors.

 A lot and as well

'A lot' and 'as well' are both two-word phrases. Make sure you don't write them as single words:

There are a lot of computers available in my library, as well as the usual books and magazines.

 No, now and know

- 'No' means 'not any' or 'not one'.
- 'Now' means 'at the present time'.
- 'Know' is a verb meaning 'to have knowledge'.
  There are no films I wouldn't try now. I know that I can enjoy any genre.

Of and off

- 'Of' expresses a relationship between things:
  I ran to the top of the stairs.
- 'Off' expresses distance or removal:
  I took the book off the shelf.

Write and right

- 'Write' means 'to put letters on paper':
  I learned to write when I was five.
- 'Right' is the opposite of wrong:
  It is right for a society to work together.
- 'Right' can also mean 'entitlement':
  You have the right to a lawyer.
- 'Right' can also refer to direction:
  The car park is on the right.

Affect and effect

- 'Affect' is a verb meaning 'to influence':
  The story really affected me.
- 'Effect' is a noun that means 'a result or change':
  The verb 'sobbed' creates a strong emotional effect in the reader.

Have and of

When we say 'would have', 'could have' or 'should have' out loud, we often say 'of' instead of 'have'. Make sure you write the correct word:

The project should have tried to raise more funds. We could have charged more for parking which would have paid for the renovations.

Bought and brought

- 'Bought' is the past tense of the verb 'to buy':
  I bought too many books until I discovered the library.
- 'Brought' is the past tense of the verb 'to bring':
  I was six when I brought home my first trophy.

Exam focus

Make sure you leave five minutes at the end of Section B in both papers to check your writing for spelling mistakes. Use the proofreading strategies on page 86 to help you.

Practice

Use the correct spelling from this page to complete each of the sentences.

1 I _____ a handmade rug home from India. It was a gift from my aunt.

2 I want to _____ a postcard to my grandad. I should _____ asked you to get me a stamp.

3 You must _____ turned left when I said to turn _____ . I don't _____ where we are!

4 I shouldn't have left the ice cream on top _____ the radiator!

5 My friend Ash _____ her new bike from the shop near school.

 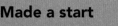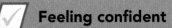

Spelling strategies

Learn these simple spelling rules to help you avoid some of the most common spelling errors.

 **Suffixes** ⑤

Follow these rules to help you add suffixes correctly to words. There are two types of suffixes:

- suffixes that start with a vowel, such as '-able', '-ed', '-er', '-ing'
- suffixes that start with a consonant, such as '-less', '-ness', '-ment', '-ly', '-y', '-ful'.

Words ending in '-e'

When you add a suffix that begins with a **consonant** to a word ending in 'e':

- You usually keep the 'e'.

  hope + less = hopeless; aware + ness = awareness; definite + ly = definitely; sincere + ly = sincerely; care + ful = careful; amaze + ment = amazement

  A common exception is 'argument'.

- However, if the suffix is '-y', drop the 'e'.

  spike + y = spiky; scare + y = scary; noise + y = noisy

When you add a suffix that begins with a **vowel**:

- You usually drop the 'e'.

  believe + able = believable; come + ing = coming

  If the word ends in 'ie' and the suffix is '-ing', drop the 'e' and change 'i' to 'y'.

  tie + ing = tying; die + ing = dying, lie + ing = lying

- However, do not drop the 'e' if the word ends in 'ce' or 'ge' and the suffix begins with the letters 'a' or 'o'.

  advantage + ous = advantageous; change + able = changeable; notice + able = noticeable

Doubling the consonant

- When you add a suffix to a word that ends in a short vowel sound and a single consonant, double the last letter.

  fat + er = fatter; slip + ed = slipped; mud + y = muddy; swim + ing = swimming

- When a word has more than one syllable and ends with the letter 'l', double the 'l'.

  cancel + ed = cancelled; propel + er = propeller; compel + ing = compelling

Challenging words ②

Try these techniques to help you spell a challenging word.

1 Look for familiar words inside the word, for example:

- there is 'a rat' in 'sep<u>arat</u>e'.
- 'science' is in 'con<u>science</u>'.

2 Say the word aloud, carefully breaking it up into syllables. Then concentrate on spelling one sound at a time: ab-so-lute-ly.

3 Make up a rhyme or saying to help you remember it.

'i' before 'e' ②

There is a rhyme to help you remember this rule: 'i' before 'e' except after 'c'. Examples include:

- believe
- achieve
- piece
- thief
- receipt
- deceive
- ceiling
- receive

Common exceptions are 'seize', 'caffeine' and 'species'.

This rule only applies when the sound represented is 'ee', so it doesn't apply to words such as 'science', 'weird', 'foreign', 'height' and 'neighbour'.

Double letters ②

It can be tricky to know which letters to double in some words. Learn the ones you struggle with. Examples include:

- necessary
- beginning
- professional
- immediately
- success
- disappointed
- tomorrow
- occurrence
- embarrass
- accommodation

c or s? ②

'Practice' or 'practise'? 'Licence' or 'license'? In cases like these where the noun and the verb sound the same, the rule is 'c' for the noun and 's' for the verb. It might help to think of similar pairings where the sound is slightly different to help you remember: 'advice' and 'advise'; 'device' and 'devise'.

I practise the guitar every day.
I booked an appointment at the doctor's practice.

Practice ⑩

Make a table of ten words you find difficult to spell, with a strategy you can use to help you with each one. Remember, some words just have to be memorised.

 Made a start **Feeling confident** **Exam ready**

Common grammatical errors

Common grammatical errors can easily be avoided by learning a few simple rules.

(5) Me, myself and I

This also depends on who or what is the subject of the sentence.

- Use 'I' when you are the subject of the sentence:
  I danced at the concert.

- If you and someone else are both performing the verb, put their name first and use 'I', not 'me':
  Billy and I danced at the concert.

- Use 'me' when you are the object of the sentence and someone else is performing the action.
  Aysha hugged me.
  Aysha hugged Billy and me.

- Only use 'myself' when you are the subject and object of the sentence:
  I'm teaching myself Japanese.

If you find this rule hard to remember, try removing the other person from the sentence. You would never say 'Me danced'.

(2) That and which

Use 'that' to add a piece of information that is essential to the meaning of the sentence:

I found the pen that I lost.

In this example, the phrase 'that I lost' tells the reader or listener exactly which pen the speaker is talking about.

I found my blue pen, which had been missing for weeks.

Here, the clause 'which had been missing for weeks' gives the reader additional, but not essential, information.

Use a comma before 'which', but not before 'that'.

Another common error with relative pronouns is to mix up 'who's' and 'whose'. Go to page 82 to revise the difference.

(2) Was and were

'Was' and 'were' are both past tense forms of the verb 'to be'. The correct form depends on the **subject** of the sentence (who or what is performing the verb).

- Use 'was' if the subject is singular and first or third person:
  I was going to the beach.
  She was about to say something.

- Use 'were' if the subject is plural or is in the second person:
  We were going to the beach.
  You were about to say something.

'Were' is also the **subjunctive** form of the verb 'to be'. Use it after 'if' when the subject is singular and first or third person:

If I were rich, I would travel the world.
If she were more ambitious, she could really go far.

(5) Tense consistency

Narrative and descriptive texts are usually written in the past or the present tense. Decide which tense you want to use and stick to it. When you're checking your work at the end, make sure you have been consistent, as changing tense is a common error. Non-fiction texts are usually written mainly in the present tense.

- Use the past tense to write about something that happened in the past:

  I looked behind me and saw a fleeting shadow in the trees.

- Use the present tense to talk about something as though it is happening right now

  As I look out across the ocean I realise how lucky I am to be alive.

- Use 'will', 'shall' or 'going to' to talk about something that will happen in the future:

  In two months I will be boarding a plane to Africa and waving goodbye to my family.

(2) Less and fewer

In speech and non-Standard English, people often use 'less' for all types of noun. However, in your exam you should use both 'less' and 'fewer'.
Use 'fewer' for:

- plural nouns

  Fewer than ten crimes a year are committed in my village.

Use 'less' for:

- things that cannot be counted

  You should use less flour in the cake.

- time, money and measurements

  I prefer to have less money and more free time.

fewer eggs
less flour

(10) Practice

Rewrite this paragraph, correcting the mistakes.

Last weekend, Laura and me went to the cinema. We was going to see an action movie but decided that a horror film would be much more fun. There was a lot of traffic and we arrive with less than five minutes to spare. The film, that was set in an underground bunker, were terrifying. Laura and myself didn't sleep at all that night!

Proofreading

Paper 1, Question 5 and Paper 2, Question 5 both test the technical accuracy of your writing as well as your language and structure. You should allow five minutes at the end of each paper to check your spelling, punctuation and grammar.

② Proofreading checklist

Check:
- ☑ spelling
- ☑ punctuation
- ☑ sense – including missing words, repeated words and clarity.

Ideally, read your work through three times, checking these one at a time.

② Aiming higher

If you have time, you could also consider the quality of your language. Ask yourself these questions:

- Can any of my language choices be more precise or engaging?
- Do I need to vary my language with synonyms?
- Do the connotations of my language choices contribute to the effect I want to create?

② Checking spelling

It can be difficult to spot spelling mistakes in your own work. Some people find it helpful to read through their writing backwards to help them focus on the spellings rather than the meaning.

Alternatively, you could skim read your response, looking for long and awkward-looking words to check.

If a word doesn't look right, try writing it in a few different ways in the margin of your exam paper, then choose the version that looks best.

② Common mistakes

Most students make similar mistakes each time they write. Look back through your work and identify which types of mistake you make most frequently. In the exam, take special care to check for these.

You could think about:

- spelling rules
- homophones
- grammar rules
- missing or repeated words.

⑤ Making corrections

Your corrections need to be clear. If you find a mistake, put a single neat line through it and add in your correction. You can do this in several ways:

- Write your correction above the mistake and draw a small arrow to it – this works well if you want to change one or two words:

> effect
> The simile has a relaxing ~~affect~~.
> ↑

- Write your correction in the margin or at the bottom of the page and use an asterisk (*) to show where it fits in – this is useful for adding or changing a longer section of text:

> Jared ~~ran~~* until he could run no further.
> *sprinted away, his trainers pounding the pavement,

- If you have forgotten to start a new paragraph, mark where it should begin with a double slash (//).

② Proofreading tips

1 Manage your time in the exam and leave a few minutes to read through your work at the end.

2 In your revision, read your work aloud, listening to the sense and rhythm. When you check your work in the exam, imagine hearing the words in your head.

3 If you come across a sentence that doesn't make sense, read it again. If it still isn't right, cross it out and try writing your idea in a different way.

4 If you still have time left at the end of the exam, check the effectiveness of your punctuation.

⑩ Practice

Rewrite this paragraph, correcting the mistakes.

> Its a grate shame that nobody thinks about the affect off their actions when they drop there litter. They would'nt behave so rudeley at home, so why do they behaved so badly in public. Just yesterday I saw a a man casualie throw a burger box out of his car windw and in to the street. Not onley was he littering, but he nearly hit an old lady wiv it!!

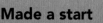 **Made a start** | 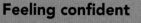 **Feeling confident** | **Exam ready**

Choosing a topic

For Spoken Language, you will need to give a presentation to your teacher or class. Choosing an engaging topic will help you to plan an engaging presentation.

② Spoken Language

Spoken Language is assessed by your teacher. It does not contribute to your overall English Language GCSE mark, so you will receive a separate grade for it.

Your presentation should be no longer than ten minutes and can be a:

- talk
- debate
- speech
- dialogue.

② Assessment objectives

Spoken Language assesses AO7, AO8 and AO9. You will need to:

- demonstrate presentation skills in a formal setting
- listen and respond appropriately to spoken language, including to questions and feedback on presentations
- use spoken Standard English effectively in speeches and presentations.

② Your topic

You can choose the topic of your presentation and must agree it with your teacher before the assessment. Make sure you pick something that interests you, so that you have plenty of good ideas about what to say. You will be assessed on your ability to answer questions, so look for a subject that will engage your audience and one about which they will have strong opinions.

You could phrase your topic as a question and consider both sides of the argument:

Why is reading so important?

Has the fashion for fitness gone too far?

Is social media a positive or negative influence on society?

Are space programmes justified, or could the money be better spent on improving the health service?

School uniform: does it bring us together or crush our individuality?

Alternatively, you could defend or criticise a statement:

School proms are an expensive waste of time.

We all have a responsibility to recycle.

Internet shopping is killing our communities.

Being image obsessed is making young people miserable.

Studying science should be compulsory at A-level.

⑩ Practice

Come up with three more topic ideas of your own, and decide which one you could make into the most effective presentation.

Planning your presentation

Planning your presentation will help you to present your ideas effectively.

 Research

Researching your topic is a good place to start. This will give you a detailed understanding of it, and provide you with evidence to support your ideas. You could do your research online or in a library.

You could look for:

- facts and statistics
- expert opinions
- background information, such as the history of your topic.

 Notes and visuals

Notes can be a helpful way to keep yourself on track and remember facts and statistics. Keep them short and simple and resist the temptation to read aloud.

You may also wish to use a slide show to present photos or diagrams. Don't spend too long designing slides though, as you will not be marked on them.

 Worked example ☑

| Introduction: Global warming: are we doing enough? |
| Background |
| • First noticed 1896 by Svante Arrhenius ◄ |
| • Now – ice caps melting faster in last 20 years than previous 1000 |
| Overview – we need to do more! ◄ |
| First point: Damage to wildlife ◄ |
| • Habitat damage |
| • Up to 10 000 species extinct each year ◄ |
| Second point: Threat to humans |
| • Rising sea levels |
| • London, NY & Shanghai underwater by 2050 |
| • Food and housing crises |
| Third point: What we can do |
| • Fly less and use public transport more |
| • Recycle |
| • Support companies with green policies |
| Conclusion |
| • Act before it's too late! |
| • What type of world do you want your grandchildren to grow up in? |

Engaging your audience

You need to show that you can engage your audience. You can do this by:

- using rhetorical techniques (go to page 67)
- giving evidence to support your ideas (go to page 42)
- clearly guiding your audience (go to page 65).

Think carefully about the needs of your audience. For example, if they will be unfamiliar with your topic, you might need to provide more background information.

Structure

Structure your presentation clearly and logically to help the audience follow it. You should include an introduction and a conclusion, and set your ideas out in clear sections in between.

Consider the sequence of your points. Place linked ideas together and show development by building up from the simplest points to the most complex ones.

Include names, dates and figures to help you remember them.

Use your introduction to grab your audience's attention and give an overview of your topic.

Break your presentation into manageable sections.

Back up your points with evidence to show you have researched your topic.

Plan a powerful conclusion. Here, a rhetorical question leaves the reader thinking about the effects of global warming.

 Practice

Use the suggestions on page 87 to choose a topic. You can use one of the suggestions on the page, or one of the ideas that you came up with. Spend a few minutes researching it and then write a brief plan.

 Made a start **Feeling confident** ☑ **Exam ready**

Delivering your presentation

You will be marked not only on what you say, but also on how you say it. To fulfil the assessment objectives, you need to deliver your presentation in a clear and engaging way.

 ② Standard English

You must use Standard English in your presentation. You should:

- use a suitably formal tone (go to page 68 to revise this)
- avoid slang and colloquial language.

① Exam focus

Watch presentations by people such as politicians, presenters and subject experts online or on TV. Think about how they make their speech engaging, and then try out these techniques in your own presentation.

 ⑤ Body language

In a presentation, body language is a powerful tool for engaging your audience and emphasising your points.

Eye contact
It is important that you connect with the audience by making eye contact. Practise moving your glance from person to person so that everyone feels involved.

Posture
Stand up tall and still, with your chin up and your shoulders back. Think about what to do with your hands – you may feel most confident holding your notes. Try not to fidget with your hair or clothing.

Facial expression
Try to look as confident as possible while you speak. Smiling will encourage the audience to identify with you and find your points persuasive. If you really don't feel like smiling, then don't force yourself – you can express your argument in a serious and engaging way instead.

Gestures
Get used to standing with your arms relaxed and by your sides. You can then bring them up when you want to emphasise a point. However, avoid waving them around, as this can be distracting for your audience.

 ⑤ Voice

Speak loudly and slowly, pausing after each main point. Make sure you pronounce your words clearly – if you have any challenging words to say, write out the sounds in your notes.

Vary the pitch and tone of your voice for effect. For example, raising your voice at the end of a sentence or rhetorical question will create a questioning tone. Alternatively, suddenly lowering your voice could create a serious tone to introduce a shocking fact.

Don't forget to include rhetorical devices to engage your audience. Go to page 67 to revise these.

② Questions and feedback

As part of your presentation you must respond to questions and feedback.

When someone asks you a question:

- make eye contact with them and listen carefully
- allow them to finish speaking before you respond.

When responding:

- take a moment to gather your ideas before you reply
- don't be afraid to disagree with your audience, but make sure you are not rude or dismissive
- ask for clarification if you don't understand a question.

 ⑩ Practice

When you have planned your speech, add notes about how you will use your voice and body language to deliver it effectively.

 Made a start **Feeling confident** 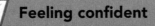 **Exam ready**

Spoken Language

Look at this transcript from a student presentation and then try the practice questions.

 Worked example

Is fast food harming our children?

Imagine a big, juicy burger and a mountain of crispy fries, washed down with gallons of soft drink and followed by all-you-can-eat ice cream. Who here can honestly say their mouth has never watered at the thought of a fast-food treat? I know mine has.

However, thousands of children in the UK are being slowly poisoned by this 'treat'. Every parent tries to protect their child from dangers such as cars, strangers and bullying. But how many think about the dangers of fast food?

When fast food first hit the UK in the 1970s, it was an exotic treat, but now it is one of our largest retail industries. According to recent research by the Department of Health, the average British child eats three takeaway meals a week. Three a week! (My sisters and I are only allowed one a month, so there must be an awful lot of children eating them every day!)

Furthermore, the research shows that up to 50% of children in Britain are now considered to be overweight. They also do less exercise than previous generations, spending hours on their phones and computers instead. And what do parents give them as a treat or reward? Junk food that contains more calories in one meal than they should be eating in a whole day.

Weight gain isn't the only danger that parents should be worried about. Fast food is often packed with sugar, salt and chemicals. These can lead to sudden energy highs followed by dramatic crashes, which affect concentration and mood. Alarmingly, some additives have even been found to have addictive properties...

So, next time you're tempted to order in a pizza to keep the children quiet, take a minute to think about all that salt, cheese and fat. They might complain now, but they'll thank you in the future!

Begin with an engaging opening to gain the audience's interest. Here, figurative language and a lively tone of voice create a vivid picture of fast food.

Use rhetorical questions to involve the audience. Combine this with eye contact to create a strong bond.

Use tone of voice to emphasise changes in mood. Here, this student lowered their voice to signal a shift to a more serious point.

Include hand movements to add a visual element. Here, the student gestured to the audience in a questioning manner to emphasise the question.

Use formal vocabulary to maintain a professional tone.

Research fact and expert opinions to make your speech convincing. Note the numbers in your plan so you don't forget them.

Raise the pitch of your voice to show surprise, such as in this exclamation.

Link your ideas together to show how they develop and build up to a convincing whole.

End your speech in a memorable way. Here, the student uses a call to action, prompting the audience to change their habits.

 Practice

1 Research and plan two further paragraphs for the speech above.

2 Write down two questions that members of the audience might ask about the presentation and make notes on how you would answer them.

Made a start   Feeling confident   Exam ready

Source A

This extract is a 21st-century fiction text. You will need to use it in the Paper 1, Section A pages where indicated.

Even the Dogs

This extract is from the opening of a novel by John McGregor. In this section, a body has been found in an abandoned flat.

1 They break down the door at the end of December and carry the body away.

The air is cold and vice-like, the sky a scouring steel-eyed blue, the trees bleached bone-white in the frosted light of the sun. We stand in a huddle by the bolted door.

The street looks quiet, from here. Steam billows and sighs from a central-heating flue. A television flickers
5 in a room next door. Someone hammers at a fencing post on the far side of the playing fields behind the flats.

An overflow pipe with a fat lip of melting ice drips on to the walkway from three floors up, the water pooling and freezing in the shade of a low brick wall.

Cars drive past, from time to time, their windows fogged and their engines straining against the cold.

10 We see someone getting out of a taxi parked further up the hill. She leaves the car door open, and we see two carrier bags stuffed full of clothes and books and make-up on the back seat. She comes up the short flight of steps, and bangs on the door. This is Laura. She shouts through the letterbox. She gestures for the taxi-driver to wait, and goes round to the side of the building. We see her climbing on to a garage roof and in through the kitchen window of the flat. She stands in the kitchen for a few moments. She looks like
15 she's talking to someone. She climbs out again, drops down from the garage roof, and gets back into the taxi.

Later, in the evening of the same day or the day after that, with the other flats glowing yellow and blue from behind thin curtains and pinned-up sheets, we see Mike scrambling up on to the garage roof. We hear shouting, and something being broken. We see Ben, running down the hill towards town.

20 We see Heather another morning, hauling herself up the steps and banging on the door, an opened can in one hand. She shouts through the letterbox and looks through the glass. The old woman from the flat next door comes out and says something. They argue, and Heather bangs on the door again before walking off down the hill towards town.

We see Mike, talking on his phone, his long coat flapping around his knees as he strides out into the road.

25 The streetlamps come on, slowly, glowing red and then orange and then flickering out again as the dawn unfurls. Frost forms across the playing fields and the grass verges, and is smudged by footprints and tyres and the weak light of the distant sun. Time seems to pass.

We see Danny, running across the playing fields with Einstein limping along behind him. We peer round the corner of the flats and see him climbing on to the roof of the garages. Einstein looks up, barking and
30 scrabbling at the garage door, and we hear the creak of a window being opened.

The old man in the wheelchair appears. We know him but we don't know his name. He's not even that old but it's something to call him. He inches along the pavement, gripping the wheels with hands wrapped in rags and unravelling gloves, his face twisting with the effort of each small push. Grunting faintly as he goes. Huh. Hah. Huh. He glances towards us but he doesn't stop. Huh. Hah. Huh. [...]

35 It gets dark, and light, and dark again, and we wonder whether anyone else will come. There are more of us now, and we stand in silence by the door, looking up and down the road.

Source B

This extract is a 21st-century fiction text. You will need to use it in the Paper 1, Section A pages where indicated.

The Girl on the Train

This extract is from the opening of a novel by Paula Hawkins. In this section, a woman is travelling to work on a train.

1   There is a pile of clothing on the side of the train tracks. Light-blue cloth – a shirt, perhaps – jumbled up with something dirty white. It's probably rubbish, part of a load fly-tipped into the scrubby little wood up the bank. It could have been left behind by the engineers who work this part of the track, they're here often enough. Or it could be something else. My mother used to tell me that I had an overactive
5   imagination; Tom said that too. I can't help it, I catch sight of these discarded scraps, a dirty T-shirt or a lonesome shoe, and all I can think of is the other shoe, and the feet that fitted into them.

The train jolts and scrapes and screeches back into motion, the little pile of clothes disappears from view and we trundle on towards London, moving at a brisk jogger's pace. Someone in the seat behind me gives a sigh of helpless irritation; the 8:04 slow train from Ashbury to Euston can test the patience of the most
10   seasoned commuter. The journey is supposed to take fifty-four minutes, but it rarely does: this section of the track is ancient, decrepit, beset with signaling problems and never-ending engineering works.

The train crawls along; it judders past warehouses and water towers, bridges and sheds, past modest Victorian houses, their backs turned squarely to the track.

My head leaning against the carriage window, I watch these houses roll past me like a tracking shot in
15   a film. I see them as others do not; even their owners probably don't see them from this perspective. Twice a day, I am offered a view into other lives, just for a moment. There's something comforting about the sight of strangers safe at home.

Someone's phone is ringing, an incongruously joyful and upbeat song. They're slow to answer, it jingles on and on around me. I can feel my fellow commuters shift in their seats, rustle their newspapers, tap at
20   their computers. The train lurches and sways around the bend, slowing as it approaches a red signal. I try not to look up, I try to read the free newspaper I was handed on my way into the station, but the words blur in front of my eyes, nothing holds my interest. In my head I can still see that little pile of clothes lying at the edge of the track, abandoned.

     Made a start   **Feeling confident**   ✓ **Exam ready**

Source C

This extract is a 21st-century fiction text. You will need to use it in the Paper 1, Section A pages where indicated.

The Trouble with Goats and Sheep

This extract is from the opening of a novel by Joanna Cannon, set in 1976. In this section, a girl is talking to her parents about Mrs Creasy, a woman from their street who has gone missing.

1   We all watched Mr Creasy. He stared into people's gardens, as though Mrs Creasy might be camping out in someone else's herbaceous border.

My father lost interest and spoke into his newspaper. 'Do you listen in on all our neighbours?' he said.

'Mr Forbes was in his garden, talking to his wife. My window was open. It was accidental listening, which
5   is allowed.' I spoke to my father, but addressed Harold Wilson and his pipe, who stared back at me from the front page.

'He won't find a woman wandering up and down the avenue,' my father said, 'although he might have more luck if he tried at number twelve.'

I watched my mother's face argue with a smile. They assumed I didn't understand the conversation, and it
10 was much easier to let them think it. My mother said I was at an *awkward age*. I didn't feel especially awkward, so I presumed she meant that it was awkward for them.

'Perhaps she's been abducted,' I said. 'Perhaps it's not safe for me to go to school today.'

'It's perfectly safe,' my mother said, 'nothing will happen to you. I won't allow it.'

'How can someone just disappear?' I watched Mr Creasy, who was marching up and down the pavement.
15 He had heavy shoulders and stared at his shoes as he walked.

'Sometimes people need their own space,' my mother spoke to the stove, 'they get confused.'

'Margaret Creasy was confused all right.' My father turned to the sports section and snapped at the pages until they were straight. 'She asked far too many questions. You couldn't get away for her rabbiting on.'

'She was just interested in people, Derek. You can feel lonely, even if you're married. And they had
20 no children.'

My mother looked over at me as though she were considering whether the last bit made any difference at all, and then she spooned porridge into a large bowl that had purple hearts all around the rim.

'Why are you talking about Mrs Creasy in the past tense?' I said. 'Is she dead?'

'No, of course not.' My mother put the bowl on the floor. 'Remington,' she shouted, 'Mummy's made your
25 breakfast.'

Remington padded into the kitchen. He used to be a Labrador, but he'd become so fat, it was difficult to tell.

'She'll turn up,' said my father.

He'd said the same thing about next door's cat. It disappeared years ago, and no one has seen it since.

Source D

This extract is a 21st-century fiction text. You will need to use it in the Paper 1, Section A pages where indicated.

The Kite Runner

This extract is from the middle of a novel by Khaled Hosseini, set in Afghanistan in 1975. In this section, a boy and his friend Hassan are taking part in a kite fighting competition.

1   At least two dozen kites already hung in the sky, like paper sharks roaming for prey. Within an hour, the number doubled, and red, blue and yellow kites glided and spun in the sky. A cold breeze wafted through my hair. The wind was perfect for kite flying, blowing just hard enough to give some lift, make the sweeps easier. Next to me, Hassan held the spool, his hands already bloodied by the string.

5   Soon, the cutting started and the first of the defeated kites whirled out of control. They fell from the sky like shooting stars with brilliant, rippling tails, showering the neighbourhoods below with prizes for the kite runners. I could hear the runners now, hollering as they ran the streets. Someone shouted reports of a fight breaking out two streets down.

     I kept stealing glances at Baba[1] sitting with Rahim Khan on the roof, wondered what he was thinking.
10   Was he cheering for me? Or did a part of him enjoy watching me fail? That was the thing about kite flying: Your mind drifted with the kite.

     They were coming down all over the place now, the kites, and I was still flying. I was still flying. My eyes kept wandering over to Baba, bundled up in his wool sweater. Was he surprised I had lasted as long as I had? *You don't keep your eyes to the sky, you won't last much longer.* I snapped my gaze back to
15   the sky. A red kite was closing in on me–I'd caught it just in time. I tangled a bit with it, ended up besting him when he became impatient and tried to cut me from below.

     Up and down the streets, kite runners were returning triumphantly, their captured kites held high. They showed them off to their parents, their friends. But they all knew the best was yet to come. The biggest prize of all was still flying. I sliced a bright yellow kite with a coiled white tail. It cost me
20   another gash on the index finger and blood trickled down into my palm. I had Hassan hold the string and sucked the blood dry, blotted my finger against my jeans.

     Within another hour, the number of surviving kites dwindled from maybe fifty to a dozen. I was one of them. I'd made it to the last dozen. I knew this part of the tournament would take a while, because the guys who had lasted this long were good–they wouldn't easily fall into simple traps like the old lift-and-
25   dive, Hassan's favourite trick.

     By three o'clock that afternoon, tufts of clouds had drifted in and the sun had slipped behind them. Shadows started to lengthen. The spectators on the roofs bundled up in scarves and thick coats. We were down to a half dozen and I was still flying. My legs ached and my neck was stiff. But with each defeated kite, hope grew in my heart, like snow collecting on a wall, one flake at a time.

30   My eyes kept returning to a blue kite that had been wreaking havoc for the last hour.

     "How many has he cut?" I asked.

     "I counted eleven," Hassan said.

     "Do you know whose it might be?"

     Hassan clucked his tongue and tipped his chin. That was a trademark Hassan gesture, meant he had
35   no idea. The blue kite sliced a big purple one and swept twice in big loops. Ten minutes later, he'd cut another two, sending hordes of kite runners racing after them.

     After another thirty minutes, only four kites remained. And I was still flying. It seemed I could hardly make a wrong move, as if every gust of wind blew in my favour. I'd never felt so in command, so lucky. It felt intoxicating. I didn't dare look up to the roof. Didn't dare take my eyes off the sky. I had to concentrate,
40   play it smart. Another fifteen minutes and what had seemed like a laughable dream that morning had suddenly become reality: It was just me and the other guy. The blue kite.

     Baba[1] – father

Made a start   Feeling confident   Exam ready

Source E

This extract is a 20th-century fiction text. You will need to use it in the Paper 1, Section A pages where indicated.

The God of Small Things

This extract is from the opening of a novel by Arundhati Roy, set in India. In this section, a woman named Rahel has returned to her family home after being away for many years.

1   May in Ayemenem is a hot, brooding month. The days are long and humid. The river shrinks and black crows gorge on bright mangoes in still, dustgreen trees. Red bananas ripen. Jackfruits burst. Dissolute bluebottles hum vacuously in the fruity air. Then they stun themselves against clear windowpanes and die, fatly baffled in the sun.

5   The nights are clear but suffused with sloth and sullen expectation.

But by early June the south-west monsoon breaks and there are three months of wind and water with short spells of sharp, glittering sunshine that thrilled children snatch to play with. The countryside turns an immodest green. Boundaries blur as tapioca fences take root and bloom. Brick walls turn mossgreen. Pepper vines snake up electric poles. Wild creepers burst through laterite banks and spill across the
10   flooded roads. Boats ply in the bazaars. And small fish appear in the puddles that fill the PWD potholes on the highways.

It was raining when Rahel came back to Ayemenem. Slanting silver ropes slammed into loose earth, ploughing it up like gunfire. The old house on the hill wore its steep, gabled roof pulled over its ears like a low hat. The walls, streaked with moss, had grown soft, and bulged a little with dampness that seeped
15   up from the ground. The wild, overgrown garden was full of the whisper and scurry of small lives. In the undergrowth a rat snake rubbed itself against a glistening stone. Hopeful yellow bullfrogs cruised the scummy pond for mates. A drenched mongoose flashed across the leaf-strewn driveway.

The house itself looked empty. The doors and windows were locked. The front verandah bare. Unfurnished. But the skyblue Plymouth with chrome tailfins was still parked outside, and inside, Baby
20   Kochamma was still alive.

She was Rahel's baby grand aunt, her grandfather's younger sister. Her name was really Navomi, Navomi Ipe, but everybody called her Baby. She became Baby Kochamma when she was old enough to be an aunt. Rahel hadn't come to see her, though. Neither niece nor baby grand aunt laboured under any illusions on that account. Rahel had come to see her brother, Estha.

Source F

This extract is a 19th-century non-fiction text. You will need to use it in the Paper 2, Section A pages where indicated.

Domestic Servants and their Duties

This extract is from a Victorian housekeeping guide. In this section, the writer is discussing the problems with servants and the difficulties they face.

1   The servant grievance is being constantly discussed to very little purpose, simply because more people are capable of deploring an evil than suggesting a remedy. Admitting that the class of domestic servants has generally become more deficient in ability than any other body of labourers in the social scale, some allowances should be made for their shortcomings owing to the exceptional circumstances to which of late

5   years they have been exposed. To cite only one cause, the increased facilities of locomotion[1]. Formerly country girls were content to live from one year's end to another in the same situations from sheer inability to defray[2] the expenses of travelling any distance. Now-a-days, railway trains have thrown the servant-market open and, consequently, even remote provinces are drained of household help. The rush is to large towns, and especially to London, where wages are high, and dress and pleasures plentiful

10 and cheap. Arrived at their destination servant girls very likely find their mistresses unable or unwilling to help them.

It used not to be so. Middle-class employers did not always consider it beneath them to engage practically in the work of housekeeping. But since the frenzy for display[3] and excitement has seized upon all classes alike, mistresses are apt to impose upon their servants responsibilities which the latter are unfitted by

15 previous training to discharge[4]. Nothing is more natural than that vexations[5] and disappointments should be the result.

It is not to be expected that any sensible change for the better will take place yet awhile. Not until education proper has corrected the existing false notions of employer and employed, may we hope for a happier state. In the meanwhile, every mistress has it in her power to help the good time in coming, by

20 fulfilling her own part of the contract with her servants scrupulously and diligently[6].

The first step in this direction is, as far as possible, to make no engagements[7] which do not promise to be of a lasting nature. By this is meant, not to engage a servant with a known unfitness for the place. Many ladies are prone to take young women into their service, just to stop a gap, or to tide over a difficulty. All that they want is, to find some one to fill the place for a time, whilst they are suiting

25 themselves at leisure.

Of course it will be remarked, that it is impossible to do the work oneself, and that the risk must be run. To this it may be replied, that it should be every mistress's endeavour to acquaint herself with "servants' work" generally, in order to meet such emergencies. If ladies were supposed to possess this knowledge more generally than is commonly believed, servants would be less independent. And for this reason like

30 other workers, they have to live by the demand for their services. As it is at present, cooks that know nothing of cookery, and nurses that are ignorant of the nurture of childhood, get as good places, and oftentimes higher wages, than women who really know their business, and are high principled enough to do what they undertake.

locomotion[1] – moving from one place to another

defray[2] – pay for

display[3] – showing off wealth

discharge[4] – complete their duties

vexations[5] – annoyances

scrupulously and diligently[6] – carefully and thoroughly

engagements[7] – formal agreements

 Made a start   **Feeling confident**   ✓ **Exam ready**

Source G

This extract is a 21st-century non-fiction text. You will need to use it in the Paper 2, Section A pages where indicated.

My Shameful Little Secret

This is an extract from a 21st-century article written for the Sunday supplement in a national broadsheet newspaper. In this section, the writer discusses modern servants.

1   Lean in and listen carefully. I have a secret to admit. One of those secrets that lurks just below the surface emerging only to spiral you down into an abyss of prickly, sweaty shame.

I used to employ somebody to clean my bathroom and kitchen every weekday.

5   Yes. Every day. That's five times a week. Every week. Then, after the bathroom and kitchen had been spritzed, they did the ironing, before knocking up a meal that wouldn't have looked out of place in a five-star restaurant. And that was just for the children.

But before you start tut-tutting – after all, I'm only a jobbing journo, not foreign royalty – be honest. Do you do your own cleaning and ironing? Because according to a new survey, over 80% of the middle-classes prefer to pay somebody else to do these tiresome chores.

10   Back in the 90s it was possible to do this cheaply by employing 'au pairs'. Foreign students taking a gap year and wanting to learn English would live in your house and do housework and childcare for up to 30 hours a week in return for room, board and pocket money. For about five years, a succession of bright, enthusiastic young women from all over the world dumped their rucksacks in our spare room, introduced themselves to our children, and began to monopolise our only bathroom.

15   Not all were wonderful; at least two spent more time speaking to their boyfriends on our phone than they did tending to the children, and one left my youngest outside in the rain as punishment for face-painting with her new lipstick. But when it worked it was a win-win situation. The girls experienced another country, made new friends and went back home fluent in English; I got my ironing done and our children learnt to say 'I don't like peas' in a variety of different languages.

20   I employed my au pairs through legitimate agencies and paid above the going rate; not just because I wanted them to be happy but also because paying more helped assuage the guilt I felt about employing a 'servant'. I was also pretty rubbish at the whole 'mistress/servant' dynamic and never felt comfortable issuing orders; many a morning found me creeping around keeping the children quiet while the au pair slept off another heavy night of partying.

25   But things have changed. It appears any sense of shame or guilt has long gone. The British middle classes now employ an army of servants to do their dirty work. Although some prefer the term 'help' as it sounds less like slavery and more like an equitable relationship.

The vast majority of this 'help' comes from Eastern Europe. They cook, clean, childmind, wash, iron and dog-walk across the land, but mainly they are to be found in large cities. Lured there no doubt by the
30   prospect of a better life, they find instead long hours of drudgery working below minimum wage for employers who can't even be bothered to learn their names. One of my neighbours wears out her cleaners faster than I wear out shoes, and refers to them all as 'the girl'.

We should be ashamed. Many of these 'girls' are highly educated. Most have better qualifications than their British employers. Many of them are more motivated, aspirational and hard-working than our own
35   young people. The same report that suggests the middle classes feel they are too posh to push a hoover claims that over half of our young people leave university unable to launder their own bedding.

Instead of subbing out our dirty work we should teach our children to wield a mop and bucket, show them how to sort a mixed wash and withhold any privileges until they have emptied the dishwasher. But most of all we should engender within them a healthy respect for those who do domestic chores. That way, if they
40   are too busy or just too plain lazy to change their own bedlinen, they might at least pay their 'girl' a decent living wage and do her the courtesy of learning her name.

Source H

This extract is a 19th-century non-fiction text. You will need to use it in the Paper 2, Section A pages where indicated.

The Murderer Hanged on the Sussex Downs

This is an extract from an article written for a broadsheet newspaper in 1881. It describes the hanging of a criminal named Lefroy.

1   Just as the clock was striking half past eight this morning the little wicket gate of the lodge of Lewes jail was opened by a warder for the purpose of admitting some dozen and a half gentlemen who till then had lingered in the garden which belongs to the prison. A bright sunshine had succeeded a gusty night, and was rapidly driving away the mists that still hung over the South Down hills.

5   At last we came to the yard – the one for which we were particularly bound – a large irregular space, bounded on one side by the prison, and on three others by high walls, and containing at one end a row of celery trenches carefully banked up. At the end, however, facing that where the vegetables were grown, and closest to the corner of the prison, were two objects which forced themselves upon the view. In the right-hand corner as we looked upon them rose a couple of thick black posts, with a huge cross piece,
10   from which dangled a staple and a long, thick rope; in the other, about 10 yards distance, an open grave.

As we filed into the yard, I noticed that we were being one by one saluted by a somewhat diminutive man clothed in brown cloth, and bearing in his arms a quantity of leather straps. There was nothing apparently in common between the grave and the gallows and the man, and for the moment I imagined that the individual who raised his hat and greeted each arrival with a "good morning, gentlemen" was a groom who
15   had chanced to pass through the place, bearing a horse's bridle and headgear, and who was anxious to be civil. But to my horror, the man in the brown coat proved to be no stranger wandering about in the manner I had pictured, but the designer of the horrible structure on the right, and the official most closely connected with that and the open grave. William Marwood it was who thus bade us welcome, and the straps on his arms were nothing less than his "tackle".

20   I confess to a shudder as I looked upon the girdle and arm pieces that had done duty on so many a struggling wretch, and half expected that the man who carried them would have attempted to hide them. But no such thing! To him they were implements of high merit, and together with the gallows formed what he now confidentially informed his hearers was "an excellent arrangement". It was evident that in the gallows and the tackle too he had more than a little pride. He was even ready to explain with much
25   volubility the awful instruments of his craft.

"That rope that you see there," quoth he, as he gazed admiringly at the crossbar of black wood, "is two and a half inches round. I've hung nine with it, and it's the same I used yesterday." Nor does he manifest the quaver of a muscle as he went on to point to certain peculiarities of design in his machinery of death. Had he been exhibiting a cooking apparatus, a patent incubator, or a corn mill, he could not have been
30   more complacent or more calm. "It's the running noose, you see," said he, "with a thimble that fits under the chin."

Source I

This extract is a 21st-century non-fiction text. You will need to use it in the Paper 2, Section A pages where indicated.

Letter to the Ashington Mail

This 21st-century source is a letter to a local newspaper. It discusses improvements to a nearby prison.

1   Dear Sir/Madam,

I am writing on behalf of the Ashington Community Action Group to express our support for the proposed improvements to Ashington Prison. Although the plans have been presented very negatively in your newspaper, many local people are strongly in favour of this compassionate, practical new approach
5   to rehabilitation.

Statistics show that the current prison system is failing its inmates. A recent study found that nearly 80% experience difficulties in finding employment after they are released from prison, and sadly nearly one in four will reoffend within a year. Clearly keeping men and women caged like animals is not the answer.

We are pleased to see that the plans for Ashington Prison include six fully-equipped modern classrooms.
10   Many vulnerable people are driven to crime by desperation and poverty, so education is a vital element of rehabilitation. These high-quality facilities will help offenders nurture and develop the skills they need to find work and build new lives for themselves once released. By making a small investment in education, the prison will greatly reduce the risk of those in its care committing crimes again – and surely a reduction in crime rates is something that all of us want.

15   There has been much complaint about the improvements to the recreational areas of the prison, but how would you feel locked in a tiny cell twenty hours a day, with no means to exercise, express yourself or even have a conversation with another human being? Experts believe that up to 75% of prison inmates suffer from mental health issues, which must surely be exacerbated by their poor quality of life. Treating them this way is barbaric and certainly won't help them reintegrate into the community.

20   Finally, we are shocked by your newspaper's scare-mongering response to the prison's proposed community outreach programme. It is irresponsible of you to print such exaggerated and biased reports as facts. Similar programmes in northern Europe have proven to be resoundingly successful and actually cheaper than conventional methods. The most important thing we can do for the inmates is to allow them to share in our community life, so that they can feel less isolated, less alone. To this end, the Community
25   Action Group will be devoting all of its fundraising activities this year to supporting this honourable project.

Your journalists seem to believe that prison is all about punishment, but in this day and age it should be about support, development and reintegration. And if they cannot find it in their hearts to sympathise with the inmates at Ashington, they should at least consider the benefits of lower long-term prison costs and a reduction in crime.

30   Best wishes,

Molly Anson

Source J

This extract is a 19th-century non-fiction text. You will need to use it in the Paper 2, Section A pages where indicated.

How to Be a Lady

This is an extract from an American 19th-century guide for young women about manners. In this section, the writer discusses table manners.

1   Did it ever occur to you to inquire why all civilized people have their food prepared at particular hours, and all the family sit at table together? Why not have the food prepared, and placed where every one can go and eat, whenever he pleases, by himself? One great advantage of having a whole family sit together, and partake of their meals at the same time, is, that it brings them together in a social way, every day. But for

5   this, and the assembling of the family at prayers, they might not all meet at once for a long time. In a well-regulated family, also, it is a means of great improvement, both of mind and manners. It is, in fact, a school of good manners. You will perceive, then, how very important it is, that your behavior at table should always be regulated by the rules of propriety. If you acquire vulgar habits here, or practise rudeness, you will find it difficult to overcome them; and they will make you appear to great disadvantage.

10 I shall mention a few things to be observed, at the table, by one who would maintain a character for good breeding. And, first of all, be not tardy[1] in taking your place at the table. In a well-regulated family, the master of the family waits till all are seated before he asks a blessing.

When called to a meal, never wait to finish what you are doing, but promptly leave it, and proceed to your place. Above all, do not delay till after the blessing, and so sit down to your food like a heathen.

15 The table is a place for easy, cheerful, social intercourse; but some children make it a place of noisy clamor. It does not appear well for a very young person to be forward and talkative at table.

You should generally wait till you are spoken to; or, if you wish to make an inquiry or a remark, do it in a modest, unassuming way, not raising your voice, nor spinning out a story. And be especially careful not to interrupt any other person. Sensible people will get a very unfavorable impression concerning you, if they

20 see you bold and talkative at table. Yet you should never appear inattentive to what others are saying.

By cultivating a close observation, and studying to know and anticipate the wants of others, you will be able to do things in a genteel and graceful manner, without appearing obtrusive or forward.

Study propriety. If asked what you will be helped to, do not answer in an indefinite manner, saying, you

25 "have no choice;" for this will put the master of the house to the inconvenience of choosing for you. Do not wait, after you are asked, to determine what you will have, but answer promptly; and do not be particular in your choice. To be very particular in the choice of food is not agreeable to good breeding. Never ask for what is not on the table. Do not make remarks respecting the food; and avoid expressing your likes and dislikes of particular articles. One of your age should not appear to be an epicure.

30 Show your praise of the food set before you, by the good nature and relish with which you partake of it; but do not eat so fast as to appear voracious. Never put on sour looks, nor turn up your nose at your food. This is unmannerly, and a serious affront to the mistress of the table. Be careful to use your knife and fork as other people do, and to know when to lay them down, and when to hold them in your hands. Be careful not to drop your food, nor to spill liquids on the cloth. Do not leave the table before the family withdraw

35 from it, unless it is necessary; and then, ask to be excused. Neither linger to finish your meal, after you perceive the rest have done.

tardy[1] – a colloquialism for late

Source K

This extract is a 21st-century non-fiction text. You will need to use it in the Paper 2, Section A pages where indicated.

Why teaching table manners can do more harm than good

This is an extract from a 21st-century article written for a broadsheet newspaper. In it, the writer discusses her opinions about teaching children table manners.

1 It might be messy, but children should play with their food to stop them becoming fussy eaters. What are your rules at mealtimes?

My seven-year-old daughter has a friend round for dinner. They're pretending that raspberries are lipstick and squidging them against their lips, with lots of giggles and red-stained fingers. I could object. Instead, I
5 smile and start loading the dishwasher.

It's not that I think table manners are entirely unimportant. I have no intention of raising slurpy, finger-licking, face-smearing chimps. But I've always instinctively felt that if I wanted my children to grow up with a positive, happy, healthy, adventurous attitude to food, nagging them from a young age to behave like mini adults at the dinner table was going to be counterproductive. Not only would it create tensions at
10 the table, it would crush their enthusiasm and open-mindedness towards food pretty damn quickly.

My own childhood memories of mealtimes are still marred by my mum constantly pestering me to hold my knife right and telling me off for sculpting faces in my Angel Delight with my spoon. No, if I wanted my children to explore food by eating it, I was going to have to relax and let them explore it in any other ways, too.

15 Food is, after all, multisensory. It doesn't appeal to us through taste alone. The smell of freshly baking bread can sell houses. The colour of the inside of a perfectly ripe avocado is good enough to be painted on living room walls. And the snap of a carrot stick is a rather satisfying sound. A young child learns about the world directly through their senses. Just as a five- or six-month-old puts toys in their mouth as part of their developmental process, so babies and toddlers naturally want to touch food, feel it, squidge it,
20 squelch it, sniff it and see what noises it makes. It's not a substitute for eating, or a distraction from it. It's an important part of learning to love food and to be comfortable around it.

Anna Groom is a lead NHS paediatric dietitian. She works with children who are "selective eaters" (fussy beggars to you and me) on a daily basis. "It's really important to let children explore the sensory side of food as a whole – not just what it tastes like," she says. "It makes it more familiar to them. It makes them
25 feel 'safe' with it." The idea is that they are more likely to try it, and less likely to become fussy.

She points out that the emphasis on keeping everything clean and tidy and under control at mealtimes often starts at weaning. Watch many a parent feeding her baby and notice how they scrape the spoon around the baby's mouth after each mouthful, how they hold the bowl at arm's reach when the baby swipes for it eagerly. Yet exposure to a food, she explains – any exposure – is a vital first step, whether
30 the child eats it or not. "When I work with children who have become phobic about a particular food, I get them to draw it, touch it, play with it, smell it, kiss it, lick it!"

So – even at age seven – I will continue to let my daughter mould sand dunes out of her rice, make a clown's nose out of cherry tomato or put a blob of peanut butter on her boiled egg just to see what it tastes like. I am teaching her table manners, but I'm doing it gradually and gently. In fact, I believe it has
35 the most impact when I talk to her about them away from the table, when she's not hungry and trying to enjoy her food. The other day, as she was engrossed in using her fork to make fossil patterns in her mashed potato, she looked up and said: "You know Mummy, I wouldn't do this if I was in a restaurant."

My other child is now 14. He has always eaten everything and anything that comes his way, with the exception of raw tomato. How are his table manners? Pretty good. I've noticed he still likes to have a
40 (discreet) animalistic sniff of a frankfurter before he puts it in his mouth, but he knows how to eat politely.

Source L

This extract is a 19th-century non-fiction text. You will need to use it in the Paper 2, Section A pages where indicated.

Around the World in Seventy-Two Days

In 1889, the journalist Nellie Bly set a new world record by travelling around the world in 72 days. In this extract from her account of the journey, she describes her thoughts and feelings as she sets off alone on her travels.

1   The last moment at home came. There was a hasty kiss for the dear ones, and a blind rush downstairs trying to overcome the hard lump in my throat that threatened to make me regret the journey that lay before me.

"Don't worry," I said encouragingly, as I was unable to speak that dreadful word, goodbye; "only think of me
5   as having a vacation and the most enjoyable time in my life."

Then to encourage myself I thought, as I was on my way to the ship: "It's only a matter of 28,000 miles, and seventy-five days and four hours, until I shall be back again."

A few friends who told of my hurried departure, were there to say good-bye. The morning was bright and beautiful, and everything seemed very pleasant while the boat was still; but when they were warned to go
10   ashore, I began to realize what it meant for me.

"Keep up your courage," they said to me while they gave my hand the farewell clasp. I saw the moisture in their eyes and I tried to smile so that their last recollection of me would be one that would cheer them.

But when the whistle blew and they were on the pier, and I was on the Augusta Victoria[1], which was slowly but surely moving away from all I knew, taking me to strange lands and strange people, I felt lost. My head
15   felt dizzy and my heart felt as if it would burst. Only seventy-five days! Yes, but it seemed an age and the world lost its roundness and seemed a long distance with no end, and – well, I never turn back.

I looked as long as I could at the people on the pier. I did not feel as happy as I have at other times in life. I had a sentimental longing to take farewell of everything.

"I am off," I thought sadly, "and shall I ever get back?"

20   Intense heat, bitter cold, terrible storms, shipwrecks, fevers, all such agreeable topics had been drummed into me until I felt much as I imagine one would feel if shut in a cave of midnight darkness and told that all sorts of horrors were waiting to gobble one up.

The morning was beautiful and the bay never looked lovelier. The ship glided out smoothly and quietly, and the people on deck looked for their chairs and rugs and got into comfortable positions, as if
25   determined to enjoy themselves while they could, for they did not know what moment someone would be enjoying themselves at their expense.

When the pilot[2] went off everybody rushed to the side of the ship to see him go down the little rope ladder. I watched him closely, but he climbed down and into the row boat, that was waiting to carry him to the pilot boat, without giving one glance back to us. It was an old story to him, but I could not help
30   wondering if the ship should go down, whether there would not be some word or glance he would wish he had given.

"You have now started on your trip," someone said to me. "As soon as the pilot goes off and the captain assumes command, then, and only then our voyage begins, so now you are really started on your tour around the world."

35   Something in his words turned my thoughts to that demon of the sea – sea-sickness.

Augusta Victoria[1] – the ship on which Bly began her journey

pilot[2] – the person who steers a ship out of the harbour

 Made a start   Feeling confident   Exam ready

Source M

This extract is a 21st-century non-fiction text. You will need to use it in the Paper 2, Section A pages where indicated.

Travelling to Birmingham

This is an extract from an article in a 21st-century online magazine. In it, the author discusses his opinions about travel.

1   Travelling is actually a state of mind that involves being open to other cultures and having a permanent sense of curiosity. A short summer holiday doesn't cut the mustard as this sense of curiosity can't be satisfied with resorts, museums and tourist attractions.

5   Many years passed before I realised you can "travel" in your own country, that we are actually surrounded by exotic locations, places we've never seen and dialects we don't understand. I sometimes do this by hitchhiking, cycle touring and visiting places outside my comfort zone.

     Every year I take my kids on holiday to Scotland and this year I have a new plan - to show them at least one British city on the way north from Luton Airport. This year I decided to take them to Birmingham and stay in a hostel. They were fine about Birmingham but went on strike about staying in a hostel ("how can
10   we share a room with strangers?" they wailed). In the end I gave up on the hostel, realizing that getting other people out of their comfort zones is damned hard.

     I posted my plan to visit Birmingham on Twitter and got a post from an English playwright called Sophia Sheridan who asked why a wannabe travel writer like myself would be visiting a place like Birmingham (note to non-British readers: Birmingham has the reputation of being a boring, ugly dump that's best
15   avoided).

     I replied to my new found Twitter friend that I'm visiting England's second biggest city precisely because it's not somewhere a visitor to the UK would normally visit (cities like Oxford, Cambridge, Bristol, Edinburgh and St Andrews are the recommended locations).

     Sophia's reply - "I can't wait to read your impressions" - was all the stimulus I needed for writing this
20   article".

     Birmingham blew me away. The city centre is beautiful. I didn't recognize it from the concrete jungle I visited several times in the 80s and 90s. A featureless city centre that was dominated by motorways and concrete blocks has been transformed into a charming series of pedestrian zones, parks and canals - with beautifully restored old buildings (where were they in the 80s?) and stunning new architecture.

25   We saw thousands of people with roots in the Middle East and Asia and I remember my friend Mario, whose mother was an Italian immigrant who ran a Greasy Spoon café in the centre of town, and realised that Birmingham is a big melting pot. It would be a great place to explore, much more interesting than those pretty university towns mentioned above which seem to be overpopulated by tourists and rich students.

Answers

Analysing fiction

Page 1 Types of fiction text
Your own answer.

Page 2 Explicit information
Answers should quote and/or paraphrase four things from the source. For example:
- Journalists are talking.
- News reports are being recorded.
- Reporters are drinking coffee.
- Vans with satellite dishes are parked.

Page 3 Paper 1, Question 1
Grade 5–6 answer (three correct things identified):
- A phone is ringing.
- Commuters are shifting in their seats.
- People are reading newspapers.

Grade 8–9 answer (four correct things identified):
- A phone is ringing.
- Commuters are shifting in their seats.
- People are reading newspapers.
- People are using computers.

Page 4 Critical analysis
For example:

The writer begins the source with a feeling of mystery. She achieves this with the strange image of Mr Creasy staring into people's gardens. His unusual behaviour implies that Mrs Creasy is missing. This intrigues readers so that they want to read on. They know that a woman is missing, but have no idea what has happened to her.

Page 5 Word classes
For example:
a) 'Captured' is used as an adjective to describe the kites. This implies violence, mirroring the dramatic kite fight going on in the sky. It also emphasises ownership, suggesting how proud the kite runners are of them.
b) The adverb 'triumphantly' describes the way the kite runners move. It suggests a powerful victory, drawing the reader's attention back to the kite fight.

Page 6 Words and phrases
Answers might include:
- The adjectives 'dirty white' and the noun 'rubbish' suggest how grimy the scene is.
- The noun 'pile' and the verbs 'jumbled' and 'discarded' suggest that people carelessly dump rubbish here.
- 'Scrubby little wood' implies that even the nature in the scene outside the window is unattractive.

Page 7 Inference
Answers might include:
- Inference: The narrator works in London.

  Evidence: She is on a 'commuter' train to 'Euston'. She also knows that it often takes longer than it should, suggesting she catches that specific train regularly.
- Inference: She is very aware of her surroundings.

  Evidence: She hears one passenger let out 'a sigh of helpless irritation' and hears others 'shift in their seats, rustle their newspapers, tap at their computers'.
- Inference: She finds it difficult to control her thoughts.

  Evidence: she admits that her mother told her she has an 'overactive imagination'. She also says 'all I can think of' is the clothes by the track.

Page 8 Connotations
For example:
1. a) glossy – glamour, wealth, shiny, healthy, expensive
   b) exploded – violence, noise, danger
   c) sedate – quiet, calm, peaceful, serene, dignified, dull
2. For example:

   The writer describes the street as 'sedate'. This has connotations of calm and peace, suggesting that it is usually a safe and relaxed place. 'Glossy' has connotations of glamour and wealth, which suggests that the houses with glossy doors are expensive and well cared for. These impressions contrast strongly with the violent, noisy connotations of 'exploded'. This emphasises how shocking the crime was.

Page 9 Figurative language
Answers could include:
- 'Thin ribbon' metaphor suggests something twisting far into the distance.
- 'Lapped wearily' personifies the river as tired and lifeless.
- 'Sequinned' is an attractive metaphor, which contrasts unexpectedly with the image of 'a dead fish.'
- 'Choked' personifies the river as suffocating, implying it is not healthy.
- 'Waved' personifies the roots, making them sound alarmingly alive.
- 'Like thin tentacles' is a simile that compares the roots to grasping limbs.

Page 10 Sentence forms
Answers might include:
- Short single-clause sentences in the first paragraph create a feeling of stillness and tension.
- The long multi-clause sentence in the third paragraph creates a contrasting feeling of movement and relief when the rain comes.

Page 11 Reading the question

Look in detail at this extract from **lines 1 to 8** of Source E on page 95.

How does the writer use <u>language</u> to describe the <u>atmosphere</u> at the <u>house</u>?

You could include the writer's choice of:

- <u>words</u> and <u>phrases</u>
- <u>language forms</u> and <u>techniques</u>
- <u>sentence forms</u>.

Page 12 Annotating the text

For example:

1. Carved from icing sugar – delicious, luxurious, fragile

2. In contrast, the Idzumo is described as 'carved from icing sugar'. This suggests that it is fragile, but also beautiful and luxurious. It highlights how out of reach the boat is to the narrator sitting on the dock, making us pity him.

Page 13 Using evidence

Answers should use both quotation and paraphrasing. Points might include:

- The repetition of 'we see' emphasises how many people come and go.
- The vagueness of 'the same day or the day after that' suggests that the days blur together.
- The colours of the streetlamps mirror the sunrise, highlighting that a new day is beginning.
- 'Time seems to pass' explicitly describes time moving on.

Page 14 Structuring an answer

For example:

- What: Harsh language. How: 'Vice-like' metaphor. Why: Suggests that the cold weather creates a grasping, crushing atmosphere.
- What: Ominous atmosphere. How: 'Bleached bone-white' has connotations of death. Why: Reflects the dead body and suggests that even the sunlight is threatening.
- What: Personification. How: Pipe has 'fat lip' of ice. Why: Cold weather feels dangerous and aggressive.

Page 15 Paper 1, Question 2

Grade 5–6 partial answer:

In the first paragraph, the writer uses attractive language to describe the kites. He describes their colours and uses the graceful verbs 'glided and spun' to personify them as dancers. This creates a positive, joyful image, helping the reader to understand the boy's love of the kites.

However, in the next paragraph he uses more dramatic language. He describes how the kites 'whirled out of control' and uses the simile 'like shooting stars'. This suggests the tension of the competition and the sense of danger the boy feels...

Grade 8–9 partial answer:

The writer uses unusual language to describe the kites. For example, the simile 'like paper sharks' suggests that they are dangerous and predatory. This shows the narrator's anxiety about the competition, and helps the reader to understand how important it is to him.

In addition, aggressive verb choices such as 'tangled', 'besting' and 'cut' make the kites sound like weapons. Again, this emphasises the drama of the competition, showing the boy's passion and commitment...

Answers might also include:

- Verbs 'glided' and 'spun' use personification to suggest grace and beauty, as though the kites are dancers.
- Contrasting language when kites fall: 'whirled out of control', 'shooting stars'.
- 'Prizes' suggests how the boy's perception of the kites changes when they are defeated.
- Long, multi-clause sentences create a lively, urgent tone.

Page 16 Structure

Answers might include:

- Because the focus of the opening line is the pile of clothing beside the train tracks, it becomes immediately clear that this is important. As the paragraph progresses and key elements of the narrator's personality, such as her 'overactive imagination', are introduced, the reader learns that it is not the clothing itself that is important but rather the narrator's fascination with it.
- The paragraphs shift from the view, to the train, to the narrator, then to the rest of the commuters. This creates a sense of claustrophobia and restlessness.
- A lack of conjunctions in the paragraphs creates a disjointed effect, which reflects the train's movements.
- The ending links back to the beginning, which highlights the significance of the pile of clothes.

Page 17 Openings and endings

Answers might include:

- The text begins with a wide overview of the weather in the region of Ayemenem. The description creates a slow, heavy atmosphere.
- There is a contrast in the third paragraph, signalled by 'but'. This reflects the relief when the rain comes. The atmosphere changes to one of excitement and growth.
- The scene is vividly set, but no plot or characters are introduced. This intrigues the reader.

Page 18 Sequencing

Answers might include:

- Many of the paragraphs start with a reference to time, highlighting how long the competition has been going on.
- References to the reducing number of kites builds excitement.
- Repetition of 'I was still flying' emphasises the narrator's pride and astonishment.

Page 19 Paragraphs and sentences

Answers might include:

- Few adverbs connect the sentences, creating a disjointed effect. This suggests the narrator's growing nervousness.
- Minor sentences are used for emphasis: 'The blue kite.' This creates a sense of drama.
- Short, repetitive sentences show the fast pace of the competition.

Page 20 Narrative perspective

Answers might include:

- The reader is first focused on Mr Creasy and his missing wife, which emphasises their importance.
- The perspective then shifts inside, showing the family's contrasting points of view.
- The focus on the family's discussion might frustrate the reader if they want to know more about the missing woman.

Page 21 Paper 1, Question 3

Grade 5–6 partial answer:

The writer begins by focusing on 'the body'. This grabs the reader's attention immediately, making them wonder what has happened. The writer then shifts the perspective to the street, allowing the reader to infer a little about the situation through the setting.

Next, the narrative shifts again to the people coming and going from the house. This gives the reader some intriguing clues about the victim. However, the disjointed paragraphs create a feeling of uncertainty. This creates a strong sense of mystery, making the reader want to find out more...

Grade 8–9 partial answer:

The source begins powerfully with a single-paragraph sentence. This strongly focuses the reader on the body, creating an unsettling tone that overshadows what comes next.

This feeling of uneasiness is emphasised in the next four short paragraphs. The lack of cohesion creates a disorientating effect, as if the reader is glancing around the street in fear...

Answers might also include:

- The narrative focus moves from the body, to the street, to the people on the street. This connects the people with the body, making the reader fear for them.
- Regular references to the passage of time create a sense of frustration, suggesting that nothing is being done about the body.
- The end focuses the reader back on the door from the beginning, reminding them of the mysterious body and making them wonder what has happened.

Page 22 Evaluation

For example:

Inside the train, verbs like 'jingle', 'shift', 'rustle' and 'tap' add lots of sounds to the description, capturing how irritating the other passengers are. This creates a strong feeling of frustration and claustrophobia, which makes me sympathise with the narrator.

Answers might also include:

- The narrator's inability to concentrate suggests her boredom.
- The train 'lurches and sways'. Its unpredictable movements suggest how frustrating and slow it is.
- Repetition of 'I try' suggests that boredom has worn down the narrator's determination.

Page 23 Making a judgement

Any two of:

- Dramatic language ('wreaking havoc', 'bested') is used to describe the kites, showing how important the fight is to the boy.
- Repetition of 'I was still flying' emphasises his excitement.
- References to time and the number of kites slowly build tension.
- Short, single-clause sentences and minor sentences in the last paragraph show his focus zooming in on the kite.

Page 24 Narrative voice

For example:

The writer creates a strong impression that the narrator is unreliable. For example, she clearly states that her mother and Tom said she has an 'overactive imagination', but that she 'can't help it'. This makes me immediately question whether she is trustworthy, especially as her imagination already seems to be running away with her over the pile of clothes on the train tracks.

Page 25 Setting

For example:

The writer gives a vivid description of the nature in Ayemenem. She uses lots of colours to create a strong visual image, for example, 'black crows', 'dustgreen trees', 'red bananas' and 'bluebottles'. All these different colours suggest how rich and varied the nature is there.

Page 26 Atmosphere

For example:

- Intro – agree with statement. Mysterious atmosphere makes the reader feel on edge.
- Beginning – What: Focus on the body. How: Dramatic single-sentence paragraph. Why: Makes the reader want answers, feel suspicious.
- Narrative voice – What: First person plural. How: 'we see'. Why: Makes the reader wonder who 'we' are.
- Focus change – What: Focus on people. How: Lots of people, first names imply a backstory. Why: Reader wants to know connection to body.
- Ending – What: Cyclical structure. How: Returns focus to 'door'. Why: Door a symbol of secrets. Draws reader back to body.

Page 27 Character

Answers might include:

- The narrator is focused on winning: 'The biggest prize of all was still flying'.
- 'Closing in' implies how aggressive and intimidating the other kites are, but the narrator stays calm.
- He is not distracted when another kite cuts him.

Page 28 Paper 1, Question 4

Grade 5–6 partial answer:

I agree that the description of the house makes you feel sorry for Rahel.

For example, 'streaked with moss' strongly suggests that the house looks dirty and uncared for. Similarly, the description of 'dampness' makes me think that it is cold and unwelcoming inside. This might imply that Rahel's family will not be pleased to see her.

The writer also says that the windows and doors are 'locked' and the verandah is 'bare'. This gives the impression that the house is lifeless and abandoned. Seeing Rahel's family home like this makes me sympathise with her...

Grade 8–9 partial answer:

I agree that the writer's description of the house makes you feel sorry for Rahel.

She personifies 'the old house' as wearing its roof 'like a low hat'. This implies that the roof looks unstable, but also creates the rather sad image of the house peeping from under its hat in a shy or unfriendly way. This might imply that Rahel is not welcome there.

Similarly, the writer chooses words associated with nature to describe the house, such as 'moss', 'dampness' and 'seeped'. These unusual choices suggest that the house has been abandoned to the wilds of nature, and is no longer like a home at all. This contradiction with the positive family connection I associate with homes makes me pity Rahel...

Answers may also include:

- The contrast between the shabby house and the fancy car implies that whoever lives there doesn't care about it.
- Positioning the bleak description of the house in the rain after the joyful description of the rainy season in the area creates a contrast, emphasising how sad and isolated it seems.

Analysing non-fiction

Page 29 Types of non-fiction text

Your own answer.

Page 30 Interpreting unfamiliar vocabulary

improper – inappropriate, unsuitable

depraved – immoral, inappropriate

misfortune – bad luck, unfortunate effect

bestowed – given, placed

impaired – damaged, faulty

Page 31 Skimming and scanning

The writer believes that the newspaper has been unfairly presenting the improvements to the prison. She believes that the current system treats prisoners cruelly and does not help them change their behaviour. She claims that spending on the prison will save money in the long run by reducing the number of prisoners who reoffend.

Page 32 Paper 2, Question 1

Grade 5–6 answer (three correct statements identified):

B. The writer feels that meal times should be a social event.

D. The writer believes that having bad table manners creates a bad impression.

E. The writer thinks that if families did not eat and pray together they would rarely all be together.

Grade 8–9 answer (four correct statements identified):

B. The writer feels that meal times should be a social event.

D. The writer believes that having bad table manners creates a bad impression.

E. The writer thinks that if families did not eat and pray together they would rarely all be together.

H. The writer thinks that the dinner table is a place where good manners can be taught.

Page 33 Synthesising two texts

Any three of:

- The servants in Source F are from the countryside in the UK, whereas the servants in Source G are from abroad.
- The servants in Source F are not as good at their job as they used to be, whereas the servants in Source G work even harder than they did in the past.
- The servants in Source F are not always well qualified for their jobs, whereas the servants in Source G are highly educated.
- The London servants in Source F have high wages, whereas the London servants in Source G are paid less than the minimum wage.

Page 34 Structuring a synthesis answer

For example:

Both sources discuss punishments, but they differ in their severity. Source H is from the nineteenth century, when punishments were harsher. It describes the 'awful instruments' of hanging, which will be used to punish a criminal with death. This is the most severe punishment possible. In contrast, the writer of Source I discusses the cruelty of 'keeping men and women caged like animals'. Although this treatment seems shocking to the modern writer, it is less severe than the hanging in Source H.

Page 35 Paper 2, Question 2

Grade 5–6 partial answer:

The travellers in the two sources are very different. The traveller in Source M is travelling to Birmingham, which 'has the reputation of being a boring ugly dump'. This suggests he likes to visit unusual and surprising places to find out what they are like. The traveller in Source L, on the other hand, is travelling as a challenge. She must travel '28,000 miles' on a journey that will last 'seventy-five days and four hours'...

Grade 8–9 partial answer:

The sources are written by two very different travellers, travelling in different ways for different reasons. The writer of Source M wants his children to experience and explore different cities in the UK, suggesting that he enjoys unusual holidays and wants to share the experience with his children. The writer of Source L, however, is travelling alone, having said 'that dreadful word, goodbye' with 'a hasty kiss for the dear ones'. The description of 'seventy-five days' spent facing 'intense heat, bitter cold, terrible storms, shipwrecks, fevers' implies that the traveller is going to experience a dangerous adventure alone rather than the interesting family holiday described in Source M...

Answers might also include:

- The traveller in Source L 'did not feel... happy' about the journey, whereas the writer of Source M enjoys his holiday, describing Birmingham as 'beautiful'.
- The traveller in Source L is travelling in order to get around the world as quickly as possible, whereas the traveller in Source M is travelling in order to visit interesting places.

Page 36 Analysing language

For example:

- Emotive language – 'so many a struggling wretch' (Source H)
- Direct address – 'How would you feel...?' (Source I)
- Repetition – 'girl' (Source G)
- Colloquial language – 'jobbing journo' (Source G)

Page 37 Rhetorical devices

For example:

- Pattern of three – 'pedestrian zones, parks and canals' (Source M)
- Hyperbole – 'a boring, ugly dump' (Source M)
- Rhetorical question – 'Do you do your own cleaning and ironing?' (Source G)
- List – 'They cook, clean, childmind, wash, iron and dog-walk' (Source G)

Page 38 Tone, style and register

Answers might include:

- The writer uses a serious tone appropriate for writing a letter to a newspaper, which makes her opinions sound reliable.
- A formal register ('I am writing on behalf of'), ('express our support') contributes to the tone and makes her argument sound more balanced.
- Emotive language ('caged like animals') and rhetorical devices ('how would you feel?') create a persuasive style.
- Statistics such as '75% of prison inmates suffer from mental health issues' create an informative style, making the writer sound authoritative.

Page 39 Paper 2, Question 3

Grade 5–6 partial answer:

The writer shows that she is worried about her journey by describing all the dangers she will face: 'intense heat, bitter cold, terrible storms, shipwrecks, fevers'. This sentence uses a long list to show how many dangers she may encounter, using adjectives such as 'intense' and 'bitter' to exaggerate some of them to make them sound as extreme as possible...

Grade 8–9 partial answer:

The writer describes her feelings using speech to show her thoughts:

'"I am off," I thought sadly, "and shall I ever get back?"'

The use of speech gives the feeling that she is sharing her thoughts, creating an intimate, honest tone. The adverb 'sadly' shows clearly her feelings of sadness but the rhetorical question also shows her feelings of doubt and fear, suggesting how worried she is about the journey she is beginning and the dangers she will face...

Answers might also include:

- Focus on negative thoughts, emphasised through language choice, e.g. the metaphor 'a cave of midnight darkness' in which 'all sorts of horrors were waiting'.
- Negative thoughts emphasised by contrast with the 'beautiful' morning and the comfortable ship that 'glided... smoothly and quietly'. These imply the writer's anxiety.
- The final emphatic thought of 'sea-sickness' described as a 'demon' and emphasised by being positioned at the end of a sentence, separated by a dash.

Page 40 Comparing non-fiction texts

Any three of:

- Both writers believe that criminals are treated cruelly.
- Both criticise the unemotional way in which punishment is approached.
- Both writers use emotive language ('machinery of death' – Source H; 'caged like animals' – Source I) to make the reader feel pity for the criminals.
- The writer of Source H gives an eyewitness account. Similarly, the writer of Source I is writing from her personal experiences in a community action group.

Page 41 Viewpoints

Annotations should identify that, although the writers agree that the dinner table is a good place to learn, the writer of Source J believes that good table manners are vital, whereas the writer of Source K argues that it is more important for children to develop a positive relationship with food.

Page 42 Fact, opinion and expert evidence

For example:

The writer uses paraphrasing and quotes from an 'NHS paediatric dietitian' to support her point of view. By showing that an expert agrees with her, she makes her ideas about table manners seem more authoritative, which encourages the reader to agree with her. However, her aside that selective eaters are 'fussy beggars to you and me' maintains a down-to-earth tone and positive relationship with the reader, implying that she isn't just lecturing us.

Page 43 Comparing language

Answers might include:

- The verb 'mould' and the noun 'blob' in Source K have fun, messy connotations that reflect the writer's playful approach to food. This contrasts with the formality of the language used in Source J, which uses terms such as 'acquire vulgar habits' and 'practise rudeness' to reflect the writer's formal approach to table manners.
- Source J uses direct address and imperatives ('you should generally wait till you are spoken to', 'study propriety') to create an instructional tone that the reader will want to obey. In contrast, the rhetorical question in Source K ('What are your rules at mealtimes?') engages the reader by encouraging them to consider their own point of view.
- Source K engages the senses with verbs such as 'squidge', 'squelch' and 'sniff'. This emphasises her belief in the importance of playing with food. In contrast, the formal, straightforward language of Source J suggests the writer's belief in rules and order.

- Both sources use multi-clause sentences. In Source K, long multi-clause sentences like the one beginning on line 18 are used to emphasise how enthusiastically the daughter plays with her food. In Source J, multiple clauses within sentences like the one starting on line 17 are used to make the writing more precise and detailed.

Page 44 Comparing structure

The writer of Source J concludes quite abruptly, which is in keeping with the no-nonsense style they have used throughout. This perhaps implies that the information about table manners is too important to need any elaborate rhetorical devices. In fact, the long list of instructions in unconnected sentences in the final paragraph might suggest that the writer has almost too many important things to tell the reader.

In contrast, the writer of Source K ends with a humorous anecdote about her son. This creates a cyclical structure that links back to the contrasting anecdote about her daughter with which the source began. The structure helps the reader to make connections between the two and see how the messy behaviour of the younger child will naturally develop into the 'pretty good' manners of the older.

Page 45 Planning a comparative answer

For example:

- Overview – Both suggest that punishments are cruel, but present their ideas in different ways.
- Audience and purpose – Both written for newspapers to persuade a wide audience. Similar serious tone combined with emotive language ('awful instruments', 'caged'), but Source I is more argumentative.
- Structure
  H – Chronological structure builds tension and upset. The purpose of the equipment is delayed – makes it shocking when revealed. Relies on power of eyewitness account.
  I – Different point in each paragraph, with evidence. Careful structure makes the writer seem authoritative and knowledgeable.
- Rhetorical devices
  H – Sarcastic quote ('an excellent arrangement') shows disgust subtly. Reader left to make up own mind.
  I – Rhetorical question/direct address ('how would you feel?'), repetition of an idea ('less isolated, less alone'). Strongly guides the reader's emotions.

Page 46 Paper 2, Question 4

Grade 5–6 partial answer:

The writers of the two sources have very different attitudes towards travelling. The writer of Source L is very worried and anxious about it, whereas the writer of Source M enjoys it and thinks it is a valuable learning experience.

For example, the writer of Source L is upset by having to say goodbye to her 'dear ones'. She describes 'goodbye' as 'that dreadful word', implying that she can hardly bear to say it.

In contrast, the writer of Source M enjoys being 'outside my comfort zone' because it makes him 'open to other cultures' and gives him 'a permanent sense of curiosity'...

Grade 8–9 partial answer:

The two writers have very different attitudes to travel, reflecting the fact that one focuses on a visit to Birmingham and the other is travelling around the world.

The writer of Source L focuses on her fears, suggesting that she is anxious about setting off on such a daunting journey of '28,000 miles' that will take 'seventy-five days and four hours' to complete. This use of statistics emphasises the scale of the challenge that the writer is taking on. This is further emphasised by the list of her fears, implying that she wants the reader to understand what a frightening experience it is to set off by yourself on a challenge like this.

In contrast, the writer of Source M conveys his excitement about his travels, focusing on his 'sense of curiosity' and his pleasure at discovering that a city which 'has the reputation of being a boring, ugly dump' is actually 'beautiful', 'charming' and 'interesting'. These contrasting adjectives emphasise his enjoyment in discovering a new and exciting destination...

Answers may also include:

- The writer of Source L focuses on the daunting first stage of her journey, whereas the writer of Source M explores every aspect of his travels.
- The writer of Source L fears the extremes she will face around the world, e.g. 'Intense heat, bitter cold, terrible storms', whereas the writer of Source M enjoys the experience of 'other cultures'.

Writing fiction

Page 47 Audience, purpose and form

Annotations might include:

- informal language to appeal to young audience
- colloquialisms to appeal to young audience
- engaging opening to grab reader's attention
- description to set the scene of the narrative
- young protagonist to which the audience can relate.

Page 48 Vocabulary for effect

For example:

Suddenly, I jolted awake and leapt up. I could hear something rustling outside the tent. It was huffing and growling. I was paralysed with fear and felt a shiver run through my body. Finally, I managed to reach for my torch and called out, 'Who's there?'

Page 49 Figurative language for effect

Answers should include at least two of the following:

- metaphor
- simile
- personification
- reference to the senses.

Page 50 Using sentences for effect

For example:

Finally, I reached a clear patch of floor, having edged into the room past crumpled crisp packets, old apple cores and mouldy teacups, and tiptoed through the broken pieces of one of Mum's best plates. I lifted the duvet and looked under the bed, rustling open a bin bag. A six-foot snake stared at me from behind a dirty sock. I froze. Menacingly, it flicked its forked tongue at me.

Page 51 Paragraphing

Paragraphs should be used correctly and be appropriately linked. A single-sentence paragraph may be used for dramatic effect.

Page 52 Creative openings

Answers should use dialogue, mystery, conflict or description to create an effective opening. The language and chosen technique should be appropriate for the subject matter and engaging for an audience of young people.

Page 53 Creative endings

Answers should use resolution, a cliffhanger or a twist to create an effective ending. The language and chosen technique should be appropriate for the subject matter and be engaging for an audience of young people.

Page 54 Implying meaning

Responses should use 'show not tell' techniques, such as pathetic fallacy or withholding information to create mystery, in order to describe setting and character.

Page 55 Gathering descriptive ideas

Answers should:
- include a range of appropriate ideas
- be structured using the questions on the page
- show evidence of selecting and ordering ideas.

Page 56 Structuring descriptive writing

Answers should:
- include a beginning, middle and end
- show consideration of narrative perspective
- include cinematic techniques.

Page 57 Gathering narrative ideas

Answers should include:
- a range of appropriate ideas
- consideration of plot and genre
- consideration of character
- consideration of setting and atmosphere
- a choice of narrative voice.

Page 58 Structuring narrative writing

Answers should:
- include exposition, a main event, development and resolution
- show consideration of narrative perspective.

Page 59 Narrative writing

Grade 5–6 partial answer:

It started like any other morning. One minute I was dreaming of walking on a perfect, golden beach with the sea gently lapping at my toes. The next, I was back in my cold, untidy bedroom with Mum yelling at me through the door. I was late for school again.

In my rush, I didn't notice that anything was wrong at first. I grabbed my rumpled uniform, dragged a hairbrush through my hair and leapt down the stairs two at a time.

The light streaming through the kitchen window seemed a little brighter than usual, but then again I felt like a vampire in the sunshine most mornings. In my pocket, my phone was buzzing like mad, but I resisted the temptation to check it. I grabbed a couple of biscuits and then headed for the front door.

I was out of the front garden and most of the way down the street before I realised. My school, whose boring grey buildings usually loomed over my house, had disappeared...

Grade 8–9 partial answer:

"Rosie! Rosie! You should be leaving now!"

Reality jolted me awake like an ice-cold shower. Gone were the golden beach and sighing sea, replaced with the gloom of my cold, messy bedroom. Once again, I was late for school.

I didn't notice that anything was wrong at first. I rushed about like one of my brother's wind-up toys, hunting for my school books, rescuing my uniform from the floor and tugging a hairbrush through my unwilling hair. The kitchen window should have given it away, or perhaps the frantic buzzing of my phone in my pocket, but all I was interested in were the chocolate digestives in the biscuit tin.

I charged out the door, narrowly missing the cat, and leapt over the rusty gate. Head down, I sprinted the length of the street, totally oblivious until I was tripped up by my own stupid feet.

That's when I realised.

My school, whose ominous grey buildings usually loomed over my house like a dreaded maths test, had disappeared! No ruins, no rubble, just an empty space...

Page 60 Descriptive writing

Grade 5–6 partial answer:

I couldn't believe it – we were finally here!

It was a cold autumn night, but music and lights filled the sky with a warm glow, inviting us in. We were still waiting in the queue, but the sweet smell of fresh donuts was tickling my nose already. To pass the time, I imagined the crunch of the sugar, followed by the warm fluffy middle. Next to me, my little brother Sam was hopping around like a bouncy ball. Being allowed to go to the fair was like having Christmas and his birthday all at once.

Normally, Acton Green was a flat, grubby wasteland of unloved fields, but tonight it was magical. The Screamer ride towered over the trees like a skyscraper. Below it, dodgems and spinners danced and whirled, causing the passengers to scream with delight. Tonight was going to be the best night ever...

Grade 8–9 partial answer:

I couldn't believe it. After weeks of pestering Mum and Dad, months of saving up pocket money and half an hour on the bus, we were finally here.

The funfair was like a box of jewels against the velvety black sky. Thousands of tiny lights danced and winked, irresistibly drawing us in. We joined the queue with hundreds of others – adults, teenagers and children all brought together by the dazzling sight. Already, the intoxicating scent of freshly cooked doughnuts was wafting its way through the air. It was the sweet smell of freedom, of excitement.

Acton Green was usually a scrubby wasteland of unloved fields, but tonight it was a bustling city. The Screamer was a skyscraper, towering over the trees, and at its feet food stalls and games formed busy streets. Crowds of people flowed everywhere, all seeking something special – excitement, fun, terror, even love. It was a magical place where anything could happen...

Writing non-fiction

Page 61 Audience, form and purpose

Annotations might include:

- formal language to appeal to an adult audience
- suitable language to achieve the purpose of explaining a point of view
- a greeting appropriate for a letter
- an overview introducing your opinion.

Page 62 Writing for an audience

Answers might include:

- informal language
- contractions
- colloquial language
- short sentences.

Page 63 Introductions

Example 1:

Teenagers are not known for their interest in politics, but a recent survey suggests that they are even more clueless than was thought previously. Results of a survey by the Schools Council suggest that over 85% of 16 year olds can't outline the main policies of the current government! We must act now to help them take responsibility for their futures.

Example 2:

Were you thinking about politics when you were 16? Or were you thinking about your exams, your love life and what you were going to do at the weekend?

Page 64 Conclusions

Example 1:

We must educate our teenagers and allow them to take part in politics. Otherwise, there will be no one left who can be bothered to vote in thirty years' time.

Example 2:

These young people are the future. The more they can learn now, the better they can make that future for all of us.

Page 65 Directing the reader

Answers should:

- be broken into carefully structured paragraphs
- use topic sentences to make links between paragraphs
- use adverbials to make links between ideas.

Page 66 Influencing the reader

Answers should include:

- a range of sophisticated vocabulary
- emotive language
- evidence
- a variety of sentence structures.

Page 67 Rhetorical techniques

Answers should include at least three of the following:

- rhetorical questions
- direct address
- repetition
- lists
- emotive language
- pattern of three
- hyperbole.

Page 68 Using tone, style and register

Answers might include:

- a mature but relaxed tone, suitable for a broadsheet newspaper
- a conversational style to engage the reader
- a formal register with occasional informal language for effect.

Page 69 Articles

For example:

Teenage Terrors

How much further will we let our teenagers push us?

Nowadays, parents strive to bring up confident, ambitious children. We tell them over and over again that they are important, that they can do whatever they want, that they shouldn't let anyone push them around. We mean well, but we are actually raising an army of arrogant, disrespectful teenagers who terrorise their communities.

Page 70 Letters

Answers should include:

- an appropriate greeting and sign-off
- a serious tone and formal style suitable for a letter to a headteacher
- an overview of the writer's opinion
- an engaging ending such as a call for action.

Page 71 Speeches

Answers should include:

- an engaging opening
- a memorable ending
- adverbials to help the audience follow the argument
- direct address
- emotive language.

Page 72 Essays

Answers should include:

- a formal register and professional tone
- sophisticated language
- evidence to support points
- a brief introduction
- a memorable conclusion.

Page 73 Leaflets

Answers should include:

- a suitable title
- subheadings
- bullet points
- numbered lists.

Page 74 Gathering non-fiction ideas

For example:

For	Against
• distraction in lessons	• self-expression
• bullying	• a support network
• cannot be monitored by teachers	• strengthens friendships
• lowers concentration span	• a platform for debate
	• develops communication skills

Page 75 Structuring non-fiction

Answers should include:

- the key features of a letter (appropriate greeting and sign-off)
- an engaging opening
- a carefully planned paragraph for each point
- a logical structure that links ideas and develops a convincing argument
- notes on rhetorical devices and evidence
- a memorable ending.

Page 76 Paper 2, Question 5

Grade 5–6 partial answer:

A recent study found that almost 50% of us watch reality TV regularly. So why are we still so ashamed of it? It is a perfect combination of entertainment and reality.

People are often very critical of reality TV stars, saying that they have no talent and just want to be famous. However, they never say the same thing about actors, who obviously want to be famous too. Perhaps they're jealous, wishing they could have their own five minutes of fame...

Grade 8–9 partial answer:

Do you watch reality TV? I know I do. A recent study found that almost 50% of us watch it regularly. So why are we still so ashamed of it? Its unique blend of fact and fiction manages to entertain while also teaching us about ourselves. This unique format should be celebrated, not ridiculed.

People are often very critical of the participants in reality TV shows, claiming that they are talentless and simply seeking the limelight. But perhaps their discomfort at seeing ordinary people on the television reveals something uncomfortable about their own desires and the society we live in. Secretly, we'd all like to be up there in front of the cameras and the bright lights, telling our story to the nation...

Writing skills

Page 77 Beginning a sentence

Answers should include varied and effective use of sentence beginnings, such as sentences beginning with pronouns, prepositions, verbs, adjectives, adverbs and conjunctions.

Page 78 Ending a sentence

For example:

You often hear that a dog is for life, but do the vast majority of people who repeat this cliché fully appreciate what it implies? No! Puppies are small and cuddly, but too many new dog owners fail to realise they will soon grow. After a year or more, they are puppies no longer and have grown into huge dogs needing vast amounts of exercise, vast amounts of food and vast amounts of attention. All too often the result is disaster. It's not just furniture that gets chewed and destroyed. People can be hurt by dogs that have become aggressive through lack of training or lack of care. Will we as a society continue to permit this? It remains to be seen...

Page 79 Commas, semi-colons & colons

Answers should include:

- commas
- a list
- a semi-colon
- a colon.

Page 80 Other punctuation

For example:

In his blog 'How to Stay Healthy', Obasi Okeke states that even a small amount of exercise can make a big difference. 'It doesn't matter how long you spend exercising. What matters is that you do something regularly,' he explains. Okeke's view is that we can all spare 20 minutes each morning. His motto is: 'There's nothing more important than your health.'

Page 81 Parentheses

For example:

I went camping with three friends when I was twelve. It rained solidly for four days, the tent leaked, we ran out of food (mainly because we burned everything we tried to cook and had to throw most of it away), and I broke my arm – but it was the best holiday I've ever had.

Page 82 Homophones

1. The description confuses the reader because they don't know <u>where</u> exactly the narrator is.
2. <u>Too</u> many owners spend less than <u>two</u> hours a night with <u>their</u> pets.
3. The lion shook <u>its</u> mane and ran off into the trees.
4. When did you last consider <u>your</u> effect on the environment?

Page 83 Common spelling errors

1. I <u>brought</u> a handmade rug home from India. It was a gift from my aunt.
2. I want to <u>write</u> a postcard to my grandad. I should <u>have</u> asked you to get me a stamp.
3. You must <u>have</u> turned left when I said to turn <u>right</u>. I don't <u>know</u> where we are!
4. I shouldn't have left the ice cream on top <u>of</u> the radiator!
5. My friend Ash <u>bought</u> her new bike from the shop near school.

Page 84 Spelling strategies

Your own answer.

Page 85 Common grammatical errors

Last weekend, Laura and <u>I</u> went to the cinema. We <u>were</u> going to see an action movie but decided that a horror film would be much more fun. There was a lot of traffic and we <u>arrived</u> with <u>fewer</u> than five minutes to spare. The film, <u>which</u> was set in an underground bunker, <u>was</u> terrifying. Laura and <u>I</u> didn't sleep at all that night!

Page 86 Proofreading

<u>It's</u> a <u>great</u> shame that nobody thinks about the <u>effect of</u> their actions when they drop <u>their</u> litter. They <u>wouldn't</u> behave so <u>rudely</u> at home, so why do they <u>behave</u> so badly in public<u>?</u> Just yesterday I saw <u>a</u> man <u>casually</u> throw a burger box out of his car <u>window</u> and <u>into</u> the street. Not <u>only</u> was he littering, but he nearly hit an old lady <u>with</u> it!

Spoken Language

Page 87 Choosing a topic

For example:

- Is work experience a waste of time?
- Schools must better prepare young people for their futures. The National Curriculum should focus on business, computing and technology.
- Christmas is a waste of time and money.

Page 88 Planning your presentation

For example:

Intro: Internet shopping is killing our communities

- 72% of people do most of their Christmas shopping online
- May affect local shops, but the benefits are worth it

First point: Accessibility

- Helps elderly people and those in isolated places
- Anecdote – grandma finds busy shops difficult with her wheelchair

Second point: Save money

- Online stores have fewer overheads, so can offer better deals
- Vital with rising costs of living

Third point: Creates jobs

- Jobs for delivery drivers
- People can't spend locally if they have no money

Conclusion

- Many benefits
- Independent stores still thriving locally

Page 89 Delivering your presentation

Your own answers. Notes should include suggestions about changes in volume or tone of voice, posture and gestures.

Page 90 Spoken Language

1. Answers should include:
   - carefully structured paragraphs
   - evidence, such as quotes, statistics or expert opinions
   - rhetorical devices, such as direct address, rhetorical questions or lists
   - suitable language, style and tone.
2. For example:

How can we encourage children to enjoy healthy food?

- Cook more from scratch – a homemade burger is much healthier
- Try healthier alternatives, e.g. oven-baked potato wedges instead of fries
- Have healthy snacks available

Should fast-food companies take more responsibility?

- Yes – healthier kids' meals
- Stop giving away toys with food
- Stop advertising on kids' TV

Published by BBC Active, an imprint of Educational Publishers LLP, part of the Pearson Education Group, 80 Strand, London, WC2R 0RL.

www.pearsonschools.co.uk/BBCBitesize
© Educational Publishers LLP 2018
BBC logo © BBC 1996. BBC and BBC Active are trademarks of the British Broadcasting Corporation.

Typeset by Jouve India Private Limited
Produced and illustrated by Elektra Media Ltd
Cover design by Andrew Magee & Pearson Education Limited 2018
Cover illustration by Darren Lingard / Oxford Designers & Illustrators

The right of Julie Hughes to be identified as author of this work has been asserted by her in accordance with the Copyright, Designs and Patents Act 1988.

First published 2018

22
10 9 8 7 6 5 4

British Library Cataloguing in Publication Data
A catalogue record for this book is available from the British Library

ISBN 978 1 406 68583 1

Acknowledgements
The author and publisher would like to thank the following individuals and organisations for permission to reproduce copyright material:

Page iii, 2, 8: The Cuckoo's Calling: Copyright © 2013 Robert Galbraith Limited.
Page 3, 92: Paula Hawkins, The Girl on the Train, © 2015, Transworld, UK.
Page 5, 94: © Khaled Hosseini, 27-Apr-2004, The Kite Runner, Bloomsbury Publishing Plc.; "Excerpted from The Kite Runner by Khaled Hosseini. Copyright © 2003 Khaled Hosseini. Reprinted by permission of Anchor Canada/Doubleday Canada, a division of Penguin Random House Canada Limited."; Excerpt(s) from THE KITE RUNNER by Khaled Hosseini, copyright © 2003 by TKR Publications, LLC. Used by permission of Riverhead, an imprint of Penguin Publishing Group, a division of Penguin Random House LLC. All rights reserved.
Page 9, 95: Excerpt(s) from THE GOD OF SMALL THINGS by Arundhati Roy, copyright © 1997 by Arundhati Roy. Used by permission of Random House, an imprint and division of Penguin Random House LLC. All rights reserved.; Reprinted by permission of HarperCollins Publishers Ltd © 1997, Arundhati Roy
Page vi, 10, 25, 91: Extract from EVEN THE DOGS by Jon McGregor. Copyright © Jon McGregor, 2010, used by permission of The Wylie Agency (UK) Limited.
Page 31, 93: Reprinted by permission of HarperCollins Publishers Ltd © 2016, Joanna Cannon.; From THE TROUBLE WITH GOATS AND SHEEP, a Novel by Joanna Cannon. Copyright © 2015 by Joanna Cannon. Originally published in Great Britain in 2015. Reprinted with the permission of Scribner, a division of Simon & Schuster, Inc. All rights reserved.
Page 37, 43, 101: Copyright Guardian News & Media Ltd 2017.
Page 103: Reproduced with the permission of RUPERT WOLFE MURRAY BLOGS AT WWW.WOLFEMURRAY.COM

Pearson acknowledges use of the following extracts:
Page 3: Doyle, Roddy, Paddy Clarke Ha Ha Ha; 2010 edition; © 1993, Vintage Books
Page 4, 12: Ballard, J. G., Empire of the Sun; 2005 edition; © 1984, Simon & Schuster, Inc.
Page 11: Flynn, Gillian, Gone Girl; 2013 edition; © 2012, Weidenfeld & Nicolson
Page 13, 15: Lee, Jonathan, High Dive; 2016 edition; © 2015, Windmill Books
Page 19: Doerr, Anthony, All the Light We Cannot See; 2017 edition; © 2014, Simon & Schuster, Inc.
Page 26: Wyndham, John, The Day of the Triffids; 2008 edition; © 1951, Penguin Books Ltd
Page 27: Bates, H. E., A Moment in Time; 2006 edition; © 1964, Pollinger in Print
Page 58: Albom, Mitch, The Five People You Meet in Heaven; 2009 edition; © 2003, Hachette Digital

Photographs
The author and publisher would like to thank the following individuals and organisations for permission to reproduce photographs: (Key: b-bottom; c-centre; l-left; r-right; t-top)
Alamy Stock Photo: Rafael Ben-Ari 55t, 56t, Henglein & Steets/Cultura Creative 56b, Michael Runkel/robertharding 60t, Eye35.pix 60b, Shutterstock: Svitlana Andrieianova ix, Bartuchna@yahoo.pl 52, Olena Yakobchuk 55b.

All other images © Pearson Education

Note from the publisher
Pearson has robust editorial processes, including answer and fact checks, to ensure the accuracy of the content in this publication, and every effort is made to ensure this publication is free of errors. We are, however, only human, and occasionally errors do occur. Pearson is not liable for any misunderstandings that arise as a result of errors in this publication, but it is our priority to ensure that the content is accurate. If you spot an error, please do contact us at resourcescorrections@pearson.com so we can make sure it is corrected.

Websites
Pearson Education Limited is not responsible for the content of third-party websites.